SOLVING CROSSWORDS

BRAIN FOOD~BRAIN FUN

SOLVING CROSSWORDS

BRAIN FOOD~BRAIN FUN

BERN KREISSMAN

SOLVING CROSSWORDS
SCALAWAG
A LAUGH · A WAY · A GAME™

Cover design by David Bacigalupi
Cover illustration by Molly Eckler
Interior design by David Bacigalupi and Patty Holden
Layout and production by Patty Holden, using the fonts
Futura and ITC Century

Bear Klaw Press
926 Plum Lane
Davis, California 95616
bearklaw@dcn.org

Printed in USA

ISBN-13: 978-0-9627489-4-3
ISBN-10: 0-9627489-4-3

Dedicated to Those Who Have Enriched My Life

C. Bronte's social novel = _ _ _ _ _ _ _

Suspense author Vincent = _ _ _ _ _ _ _ _

One-third of a Hardy title = _ _ _ _

Isabella Augusta Persse, Lady _____ = _ _ _ _ _ _ _

The Death of Marat painter = _ _ _ _ _

Half a Dickens' title = _ _ _ _ _

The better half of Jan van Eyck's famous double portrait = _ _ _ _ _ _ _ _

Russia's honored mathematician-poet-novelist, Kovalevsky = _ _ _ _ _

Wilde's Gray, eyeless: Homophone = _ _ _ _ _

Twain's partner = _ _ _ _

Giovanni Arnolfini and Giovanna Cenami

Dedicated to Those Who Have Enriched My Life

C. Bronte's social novel = Shirley

Suspense author Vincent = Starrett

One-third of a Hardy title = Jude

Isabella Augusta Persse, Lady _____ = Gregory

The Death of Marat painter = David

Half a Dickens' title = David

The better half of Jan van Eyck's famous double portrait = Giovanna

Russia's honored mathematician-poet-novelist, Kovalevsky = Sonya

Wilde's Gray, eyeless: Homophone = Doran

Twain's partner = Mark

CONTENTS

Preface

OMAR KHAYYAM—1100 AD

A Book of Verses underneath the Bough

A Jug of Wine, a Loaf of Bread—and Thou

Beside me singing in the Wilderness

Oh, Wilderness were Paradise enow!

SCALAWAG—2004 AD

A Book of Crosswords just beneath my <u>A</u>

    A—Forehead - In the lap: metaphorically =_ _ _ _

A Mug of Beer, A Bowl of Chips—and <u>B</u>

    B—MMM ÷ III: Abbr. = _ _ _ _

Beside me singing of the <u>C</u>

    C—Resolution = _ _ _ _ _ _ _ _

Ah, <u>C</u> is Paradise <u>D</u>!

    D—Enough, aplenty: Archaic = _ _ _ _

SCALAWAG—2004 AD

A Book of Crosswords just beneath my <u>A</u>

    A—Forehead - In the lap: metaphorically =_ _ _ _

A Mug of Beer, A Bowl of Chips—and <u>B</u>

    B—MMM ÷ III: Abbr. = _ _ _ _

Beside me singing of the <u>C</u>

    C—Resolution = _ _ _ _ _ _ _ _

Ah, <u>C</u> is Paradise <u>D</u>!

    D—Enough, aplenty: Archaic = _ _ _ _

SCALAWAG—2004 AD

A Book of Crosswords just beneath my Brow

A Mug of Beer, A Bowl of Chips—and Thou

Beside me singing of the Solution

Ah, Solution is Paradise enow!

Introduction—A Must Read

If I could go back and restart my academic career, I would be torn trying to choose between two collegiate disciplines: a biological science or a linguistics study. Biology, because I admire the natural world, wilderness, and the wild creatures of the earth—the outdoors, where I have spent a major portion of my recreational time. And linguistics, because my delight in words and word-play, my time indoors, is equal to the call of the wild. In several of my earlier books I paid my dues to Mother Nature. This work is an acknowledgment of my indoor passion and pastime and an introduction to SCALAWAG (Solving Crosswords—A Laugh·A Way·A Game), the solving system that has evolved from extensive on-the-puzzle practice. As the name indicates, SCALAWAG is designed to provide a remarkably effective solving method, with fun and sport in the process. With the exception of the preliminary and concluding chapters, all other chapters of the book, regardless of their headings, are elements of SCALAWAG.

A few grammatical liberties have been taken in the chapters which follow. For one, quotation marks have been omitted, except for a few instances to aid in connotation. Otherwise, these pages would be awash in those inverted commas. Second, in cases where examples are provided, a colon (:) precedes the examples and stands for the phrase "for example." The equal sign (=) is used throughout the text as shorthand for "the answer is:"

Lizard of the Nile: Abbr. = Croc

A source of potassium = Bananas

What the angry clone was = Beside himself

You will note that in proper crossword style, the initial letters of the clue and the answer are capitalized. In non-crossword style, for the sake of clarity, I have indicated a space between words, when multiple word answers are shown:

A cotton plant = Gin mill

Threw off = Lied to

No such space is allowed on the crossword grid even if the entry is normally hyphenated or apostrophized.

The New York Times crossword is syndicated and appears daily in 150 or so local newspapers, about 300 on Sunday. "Typically," according to an E-mail from Will Shortz, "the daily *NY Times* crossword appears 6 weeks later in syndication. The Sunday puzzle appears 1 week later." The *Times* puzzles are numbered and the four digit number is an indication of the date of the original publication: the first two digits stand for the month, the second two for the day. Thus, 0101 stands for January 1, 0115 for January 15, 0603 for June 3, 1215 for December 15, etc. That number will appear in local syndicated papers, though not in the parent paper since the number corresponds with the date of publication and is, thus, self evident. You can verify the publication date differential between the *Times* and your hometown gazette by comparing the two dates. For my town papers the difference is exactly forty-two days for the daily and seven for the Sunday.

Since the numbers start afresh every New Year's Day, you must know the year of publication if you seek a particular puzzle. Consequently, footnotes to any *New York Times* puzzle will show the number and the year to allow access to your regional paper as well as the *Times*. And remember, for the parent paper, the Sunday puzzle does not appear in the paper itself, but rather in the magazine section.

With a few exceptions, in situations where those exceptions are of no consequence, citations such as the examples above all have been derived from respected crossword sources, such as the *New York Times*, *Simon & Schuster's Super Crossword Books*, and the *Los Angeles Times*. About 99% are from such published sources.

Throughout the book I portray crossword constructors as devious devils whose main endeavor is to gull and bamboozle solvers—a "they versus us" conflict. That agon is designed simply to spur reader interest and, I admit, is wholly fallacious. We are all on the same page. I admire constructors and editors. They have done a magnificent job of keeping the crossword world fresh, informative, vibrant, and fun. No wonder we have

tens of millions of word addicts getting their daily fix. Constructors and editors, where would we poor solvers be without them?

Prominent constructors and editors are the cream of the crossword constellation, fine fellows and wonderful women all, highly respected by colleagues and solvers alike. At the zenith of this pantheon is the author, constructor, editor, and historian Michelle Arnot (*What's Gnu? A History of The Crossword Puzzle*. Vintage Books, 1981), and current star of "how to solve crosswords" publications (*Crossword Puzzles For Dummies*. IDG books, 1998, and three later sequents). I admire Ms. Arnot. I delighted in her historic account (except for the unfortunate lack of an index) and agree with the majority of her principles, but strongly oppose several of her solving strictures. That opposition is one major reason for the appearance of this work. Arnot inveighs against "Sticking in an 'S' when you suspect an entry may be plural," and "Assuming that an entry is a past participle (ends in ED) before you know the rest of the entry."[1] SCALAWAG to the contrary says "Do it, do it, do it" and for proof simply says go to any crossword or, better, any ten crosswords, and check how many plurals end in "S" as opposed to any other ending. Do the same for the past tense "ED." That's all the proof you will need—it will solve the matter for you.

These two points of disagreement may seem like small potatoes on which to base an argument but, since they appear so frequently on the grid, they constitute a major solving issue. Further, they are indicative of diametrically opposed philosophies. One may assume that Arnot's "don't do it" strictures would apply also to all the SCALAWAG tips to make informed guesses at all the words, prefixes, suffixes, beginnings, and endings which adorn so large a portion of our puzzles. On those cardinal issues, SCALAWAG maintains that Arnot is dead wrong and recommends strategies 180° in opposition to her teachings. Since her methods are the current prevailing mode, SCALAWAG is working to substitute a new puzzle tested, group tested, field tested, authority. I admire Arnot, but go SCALAWAG.

I owe volumes of thanks to generous friends whose particular areas of expertise were reflected in their comments and corrections on the draft manuscript. Dr. Gail Schlachter brought a remarkable author's and publisher's eye and a world of experience and knowledge to her textual emendations. She may lay claim, rightfully, to a large portion of the good parts of this book. Dr. Robert Wisner, cruciverbalist of note, provided a series of tips and suggestions and kept me abreast of crucial, current crossword oddities. Estelle Miller, fellow crossword traveler, discovered numerous crossword tricks, examples, and pranks which appear anonymously throughout the book. Dr. Elizabeth Molnar Rajec, polyglot, brought her language and literary talents to her emendations and to the translations which head each chapter of this work. Barbara Ellen Lekisch, research virtuoso extraordinaire and author I envy, applied her writing organizational skills to the creation of the index, and to the findings regarding the question of the true first crossword. David Bacigalupi, creative director, photographer, discovered a multitude of marvelous illustrative materials. Pat Hutchinson, web surfing wonder, sent me a store of punny words. Kathy Huntziker transformed my handwritten scrawl to legible type; Will Shortz answered all my crossword queries fully and promptly. The book owes its handsome countenance to the talents of three distinguished designers: Patty Holden, Molly Eckler, and David Bacigalupi. The librarians of the University of California, Davis, and of the Davis Branch of the Yolo County Library System are the mother lode of information, intelligence, and instruction, and paragons of service and assistance. Thanks also to Ann Dubell and her colleagues at the North Bay Cooperative Library System. There must be a special mansion in paradise reserved for retired librarians. Above all, my thanks to Shirley who edits my text scrupulously and my world assiduously.

Last word. Like many a malaprop, but for the delight and delectation of verbophiles and lexophiles, I have employed, throughout the text, unusual complex lexicology where a simple word would do just as well.

The author would be pleased to hear from any and all cruciverbalists.

Bern Kreissman
Bear Klaw Press
926 Plum Lane
Davis, CA 95616
bearklaw@dcn.org

The SCALAWAG system (Solving Crosswords—A Laugh·A Way·A Game™) has been derived from my crossword classes in Davis, and the name is protected.

[1] Arnot, Michelle. *Crossword Puzzles for Dummies*. IDG Books, 1998, p. 253.

Clio

Human fascination with words probably began when the cave man developed language, turning sounds into words. The Bible records Samson's wedding riddle to the Philistines, and Plutarch quotes a conundrum attributed to the Sphinx. The ancient Greeks used riddling as a sign of education and the early Romans played riddle games at religious festivals.

Scores of other word games developed over the years: anagrams, rebuses, charades, acrostics, and word squares made for evening pastimes. The word square is regarded as the closest antecedent of our crossword. A square is composed of words of equal length in which the horizontal words can also be read vertically. The most famous square, the SATOR square, was first discovered at a Roman excavation site at Cirencester, and the identical word form was later found at Pompeii, believed to date from AD 79, the eruption of Vesuvius.

```
R  O  T  A  S
O  P  E  R  A
T  E  N  E  T
A  R  E  P  O
S  A  T  O  R
```

This extraordinary square has been of scholarly interest since its initial discovery, and it is also a palindrome and an acrostic. Scholars believe that ancients regarded the square as a charm, a device of mystical qualities, and also as a form of recognition among early Christians.

Word games flourished in Europe throughout the 17th, 18th, and 19th centuries, and Tony Augarde[1] lists more than 25 pastimes, such as Hangman, Consequences, Poetry tricks, Rebuses, and Anagrams, which occupied the educated British population in those years. The Brits of those decades were dependent on their personal resources for entertainment, so it is no wonder that music (performance rather than audition), correspondence, critical conversation, and desk and parlor games engaged their leisure time.

Augarde is somewhat wistful and disconsolate that so many of the games have vanished from the household scene. However, with our cinema, radio, television, tapes, discs, DVDs, Ipods, video parlors, race meets, theme parks, ball games, etc., etc., it is no surprise that evenings of family charades have drained to a trickle. Moreover, all these sighs of nostalgia may be misplaced for, judging by the current American scene, newspaper readers get their daily helpings of anagrams in "Jumble," and the rebus is a daily and weekly feature of "Plexers" and "Frame Games." Word Seek puzzles such as "Word Sleuth" abound and cryptogram fans find their daily pleasure in "Cryptoquotes." The long tradition of riddles for children (and adults) is maintained in Sunday features across the country, and columns such as Marilyn Vos Savant's "Ask Marilyn" provide adult riddles and a weekly opportunity for word play. Scrabble tournaments are held recurrently throughout the United States, and the comic strips of the nation's newspapers are awash in word play for their tag lines. Indeed, "Frank and Ernest" by Bob Thaves (the very title is word play), relies heavily on punnery for its trenchant humor. *The Washington Post's* annual "Style Invitational Contest 2003" (add, subtract, or change one letter from a common word and affix a new definition) takes word play to the zenith:

Reintarnation = Coming back to life as a hillbilly

Inoculatte = To take coffee intravenously when you are
running late

Osteopornosis = A degenerate disease

The 2004 contest asks entrants to provide an alternative definition for a common word, and is equally witty. Among the winners:

Lymph = To walk with a lisp

Oyster = A person who sprinkles his conversation with
Yiddish expressions.

Pokemon = A Jamaican proctologist

Finally, as any dictionary editor will affirm, English is exploding with newly coined words. The teens of Palo Alto have proclaimed that oral congress is not real coition and have accordingly named it "Outercourse." A New York agency caring for seniors divides its charges into the "Wellderly" and the "Illderly." And a major author pushes the craft even further. Reginald Hill's *Dialogues of the Dead,* in a remarkable counterfeit of an OED entry, defines Paronomania:

Paronomania . . Factitious word derived from a conflation
of PARONOMASIA . . . word play + MANIA

1. A clinical obsession with word games

2. The proprietary name of a board game for two players
using tiles imprinted with letters to form words . . . (OED
2nd Edition).

And the web is deluged with punnery and other forms of word play, such as oxymoronic questions:

Why does "fat chance" and "slim chance" mean the
same thing?

If love is blind, why is lingerie so popular?

and punny answers:

A bicycle can't stand alone because it is two-tired.

A plateau is a high form of flattery.

Those who jump off a Paris bridge are in Seine.

So word games and word play are alive and flourishing in the United States, and crosswords have not even been covered. If we add crosswords to the mix, the number of participants is staggering, for cruciverbs are followed by more addicts than all other games combined, including bridge, poker, mah-jongg, chess, and checkers. Dr. Eugene T. Maleska's affably unaffected *Crosstalk* notes that a Gallup poll taken about 1965 estimated approximately "fifty million"[2] solvers hit the black and white grids on a daily and weekly basis. Have they since doubled to one hundred million? Probably not, but we may be relatively certain that today some sixty million users get their daily fix from as many as one thousand newspapers and scores of crossword books published serially. Simon & Schuster's Crossword Puzzle Series is now at number 240. Remarkable, since the first puzzle book, number 1, appeared in 1924.

Now, crosswords are everywhere. An observer mentions seeing them on "hats, T-shirts, scarves, ties, and accessories,"[3] and they appear in jigsaw puzzles, on socks, catalog covers, shopping guides, TV schedules, postage stamps, airline mags, wrapping paper, curtains, underwear—nothing is exempt. *The New Yorker* ran a particularly provocative puzzle[4] in which previously published cartoons, captionless, served as the clues. The missing captions, naturally, were the entries.

A similar but even greater display of crossword ingenuity celebrated the genius of Al Hirschfeld, the pen and ink artist who, for decades, captured the souls of Broadway, Hollywood, D.C., and UN luminaries in his playful line drawing portraits for the Sunday *New York Times*. A full page celebration of Hirschfeld showed forty-three portrait images[5] which, in association with its appropriate written clue, led to the answer. An extraordinary puzzle for an extraordinary person.

The crossword appears in elementary school classrooms across the country as a provocative device to teach spelling and to broaden vocabulary; and Anne Alcott even uses the grid to teach elementary math to "children ages 7–11."[6] For high school teens, Passport Books of Lincolnwood, Illinois, a publishing house devoted to language instruction, issues titles such as, "*Easy German Word Games and Puzzles*" and "*Easy Spanish Crossword Puzzles*" to teach Spanish, French, Italian, and German.

THE BEGINNINGS

The American newspapers of the early 1900s were the sole resource for news, and competition for readership among the rival dailies was fierce, immane, cut-throat, and unremitting. Every feature of the paper was designed to draw readers, particularly the amusement and commentary sections. It was a halcyon period for columnists like Peter Finley Dunne and George Ade in Chicago; Don Marquis, Frank Sullivan, Alice Duer Miller, and O'Henry in New York; and Ambrose Bierce in San Francisco. The comic strips also played a role in luring subscribers: Mutt & Jeff, Bringing up Father (Maggie and Jiggs), the Gumps, Gasoline Alley, Krazy Kat, Happy Hooligan, The Katzenjammer Kids daily, but particularly on Sunday. The Sunday editions were gargantuan, with added features such as the rotogravure picture supplement, heavy with sepia colored photos of national events, celebrities, and high society jinks such as polo matches, debutante balls, opera premieres, and symphony fund raisers.

The New York World, one of the city's premier newspapers, ran a special Sunday color supplement of eight to sixteen pages titled FUN, edited by Arthur Wynne, which was a happy melange of jokes, puzzles, cartoons, and riddles heavily overlaid by great old time advertisements for rupture cures, how to make love, overcoming bashfulness, curing a drinking habit, or removing bunions. For the pre-Christmas edition of FUN, December 21, 1913, Wynne decided to add a new wrinkle to puzzledom. He fashioned a diamond-shaped grid of interlocking numbered squares which he entitled Word Cross, provided thirty-one clues, and asked his readers to "Fill in the small squares with words which agree with the following definitions." The response was stunning. Wynne did not realize that he had unleashed what shortly was to become a tornado, an avalanche, a tsunami of devotion. His acknowledgment the following week made note of that early reaction, "The great interest shown in FUN's word-cross puzzle published lastweek has prompted the puzzle editor to submit another of the same kind."

On the third week, the compositors at *World* made a mistake and called the puzzle Cross-Word, which later became crossword, and it has remained so ever since. From the beginning, the typesetters loathed the crossword, and their aversion sparked an unending series of misspellings, omissions, mistaken clues, and constant grumbling. Indeed, the rest of the *World* staff sneered at the puzzles and shrugged grudging acceptance only because they knew that crosswords sold papers.

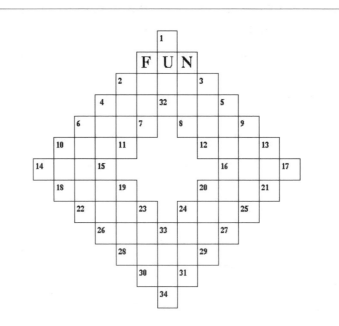

by Arthur Wynne, December 21, 1913
from The New York World

2–3.	What bargain hunters enjoy.	6–22.	What we all should be.
4–5.	A written acknowledgment.	4–26.	A day dream.
6–7.	Such and nothing more.	2–11.	A talon.
10–11.	A bird.	19–28.	A pigeon.
14–15.	Opposed to less.	F–7.	Part of your head.
18–19.	What this puzzle is.	23–30.	A river in Russia.
22–23.	An animal of prey.	1–32.	To govern.
26–27.	The close of a day.	33–34.	An aromatic plant.
28–29.	To elude.	N–8.	A fist.
30–31.	The plural of is.	24–31.	To agree with.
8–9.	To cultivate.	3–12.	Part of a ship.
12–13.	A bar of wood or iron.	20–29.	One.
16–17.	What artists learn to do.	5–27.	Exchanging.
20–21.	Fastened.	9–25.	To sink in mud.
24–25.	Found on the seashore.	13–21.	A boy.
10–18	The fibre of the gomuti palm.		

The world's first crossword

Wynne resigned as editor and selected Margaret Petheridge, a young secretary on the *Sunday World Magazine* with a newly hatched Smith College degree, to serve in his stead. Petheridge accepted the post, but continued Wynne's lax supervision of the feature and its consequent lapses. For those sins, Petheridge (supposedly) wrote that Franklin P. Adams, FPA, who had his Conning Tower column moved from *The Tribune* to *The World*, would stomp into her office every Monday to denounce the errors of the Sunday puzzle. Tired of FPA's tirades, she decided to work the puzzles herself and, consequently, to edit them diligently—she succeeded. She also brought regulation to the construction. She dropped the double number system, banned two letter words, and brought in the symmetrical diagram: that is, a grid rotated 180 degrees is exactly the same as the initial form.

After 1916, FUN was discontinued, but the puzzle, under Petheridge, marched on for a devoted band in *The Sunday World Magazine*. In 1924, two graduates of the Columbia University School of Journalism, Richard Simon and Max Schuster, opened a publishing house. A probably apocryphal story relates that Simon's aunt Wixie asked him to find a book of crosswords as a gift to her daughter, an avid puzzler. Simon discovered that no such compilation existed and approached Schuster with a view toward publishing such a work. Schuster agreed, but with dire warnings of failure from FPA and others, the partners avoided tarnishing the good name of Simon & Schuster by subterfuge, publishing the book as an imprint of the Plaza Publishing Company. They asked Petheridge to edit the work and she, along with two other *World* game editors, Prosper Burranelli and F. Gregory Hartswick, agreed to collaborate. They each received an advance of $25.00. For $1.35, subscribers acquired the book, an attached Venus pencil with eraser, and a postcard to request all the answers.

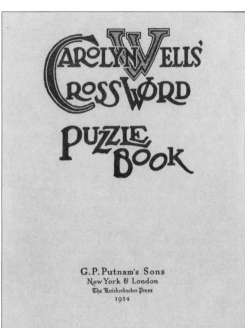

The first printing of 3,000 copies sold out in one day and nine subsequent printings followed. One year later, with three volumes in print, Simon & Schuster sold almost one-half million copies, and the office-mates were pleased to affix the Simon & Schuster logo to all subsequent printings. Also, rival crossword books were already on the market.

Crosswords shortly overwhelmed all other crazes of the day including the reigning favorite, Mah-Jongg. Petheridge married publisher John Farrar in 1926, and she is enshrined in crossword history as Margaret Farrar, godmother of all crossword votaries. She resigned from *The World* to devote herself to marriage and Simon & Schuster.

THE CRAZE

The crossword craze grew and, on November 24, 1924, the puzzle became a daily feature of *The World*; other newspapers also adopted the puzzle. Crossword stories claiming businesses were suffering from inattention and negligence by puzzlers circulated widely. A columnist wrote that the puzzles loomed as the cause of broken homes, drunkenness, and increases in all crimes. In Chicago, a judge sentenced a crossword husband to no more than three puzzles a day to save the marriage. A Broadway musical, "Puzzles of 1925," included a sketch of a rehab facility for addicts seeking a cure from crossworditis. A trio of restaurant diners refused to leave the eatery until their crossword was completed, but the police intervened. Academics sought unsuccessfully to assess the reasons for the mania.

Meanwhile, sales of dictionaries and thesauruses soared, and libraries complained that their dictionaries, encyclopedias, and related reference books were consumed to tatters. Many libraries placed restrictions on those volumes or removed them from public use. On the other hand, the Baltimore and Ohio Railroad commuter trains added dictionaries to every car for riders from suburbia to metropolis. One English journalist estimated that Americans spent five million hours a day on crosswords, most presumably on work time. *The Times* (London) noted that Americans had become "psychologically enslaved" whereas the English were too clever for such nonsense. However, unbeknownst to *The Times*, Arthur Wynne had already sold six puzzles to England's *Sunday Express*.

Nonetheless, the craze continued, and in 1941, even the magisterial *New York Times* saw the black and white handwriting on the wall, and induced Margaret Farrar to develop a crossword section for its *Sunday Magazine*. The first such puzzle appeared on February 15, 1942, and eight years later, on September 11, 1950, it became a daily feature and the most prestigious American crossword, a position it has held to this day despite excellent competing puzzles in Boston, Chicago, Los Angeles, and other major cities.

Farrar unintentionally started the *Times'* hallmark puzzle system of progressive difficulty: the daily gradation from the easiest on Monday to the most difficult on Saturday. She felt that puzzlers who had worked the large difficult puzzle on Sunday should have a respite from brain work on Monday, and

Sheet music for "Cross Words Between Sweetie And Me" published in 1925.

her Monday puzzles were simple. That easy on Monday to difficult on the weekend has been modified by later *Times'* editors to top out on Saturday. Sunday's puzzle, somewhat difficult and larger than the dailies, stands outside the scheme. In addition to other rules, Farrar decreed that only one-sixth (approximately) of the grid should hold black squares, every letter must be checked, that is, appear in two words, no two letter words, no white squares may be walled off totally by black squares, and all white squares must be contiguous.

Farrar was succeeded at *The Times* by Will Weng, editor from 1969 to 1977. He reinforced Farrar's rules and was followed by Eugene T. Maleska, the first recognized "word" authority to accept the post. Maleska brought a world of innovation: literacy, fun, wit, erudition, and intellect to the puzzles, despite the sense by some of his peers that he was somewhat humorless and contentious as an editor. Under Maleska, editor from 1977 to his death in 1993, *The Times* grew in repute and influence. On his death, a second linguistic adept, Will Shortz, assumed the reins. Under Shortz, *The Times'* crossword has maintained its ascendancy, but there are more than a score of other distinguished cruciverbalists associated with daily newspapers, monthly journals, and occasional publications. To name them all would be trying. To omit one would be an injustice. So!

THE CRYPTIC CROSSWORD

From 1924 on, crosswords had found a home in English newspapers (and continental dailies as well), despite *The Times* (London) editorial calling Americans "enslaved" and noting that the puzzles "had made devastating inroads on the working hours of every rank of society." In England, the popularity of the crossword matched that of the U.S. However, the English crossword was to make a right angle turn away from its American cousin. Under the guidance of Edward Powys Mather, editing under the anonym, "Torquemada," the English rules decreed that all clues were to be devious, recondite, difficult of interpretation, witty, linguistically challenging, and intellectually charged. Straight dictionary clues were prohibited, to be replaced with puns, anagrams, homophones, hidden words, deletions, backward readings, and several score other verbal tricks.

Under Torquemada, other rules were to emerge. Symmetrical diagrams were too restrictive, black boxes were replaced by simple word separators, each letter did not require a check, and the clue usually included two hints to the answer: a hidden, somewhat far-fetched synonym of the solution and word play leading to that response, called a light. These rules hold for the majority of English crosswords, but this sceptered isle has spawned a couple of hybrids. *The Times* puzzle, perhaps the most prestigious crossword in the world, employs a symmetric

U.S.P.S. stamp commemorating the first crossword puzzle, issued in 1998 as part of the Postal Service's Celebrate the Century education series.

cryptic grid, and the popular periodical publication, *Quick Crossword*, goes a step further with a symmetric grid and American style clues. Mather developed a sizable and extraordinarily loyal following, and he was succeeded by equally prestigious editors who carried out his basic instructions and even improved the product: Derrick Somerset MacNutt, dubbed "Ximenes;" Jonathan Crowther, "Azed;" and A.F. Ritchie, "Afrit."

The English or cryptic crossword[7] also enjoys a strong following in the U.S. It first appeared in the *New York* magazine edited by Stephen Sondheim, then by Richard Maltby Jr. It held for a period in the *New Yorker*, and has been a mainstay of the *Atlantic Monthly* under Emily Cox and Henry Rathvon, and of *Harper's* by Richard E. Maltby, Jr.

With the rise of crosswords came a glut of publications to aid in their execution: crossword dictionaries; name finders; word banks by word length or letter placement; dictionaries of foreignisms; manuals of word beginnings and endings; handbooks of synonyms and antonyms; references for pet crossword topics; tomes listing thousands of movie titles, actors, and celebrities; encyclopedias of religion, gods and goddesses; lists of everything Shakespearean: plays, characters, scenes, and events; alphabetized lists of puns and familiar phrases, etc., etc., etc.

And then along came the computer. Of enormous aid to the constructor, the computer was also set to answer any clue of any constructor. If a book could offer 100,000 celebrity names, the computer could offer one million. If a book could show 50,000 words by letter sequence, the computer could show 500,000. A published aid might list 500,000 near synonyms, the computer two million. The computer will soon be set to take the unmarked crossword in slot A and spit out the completed puzzle as slot B. But where's the fun in that? As you work your way up to progressively harder puzzles, you may some day wish to access your computer. That will be a sad day.

---

[1] Augarde, Tony. *Oxford Guide to Word Games*. 2nd ed. Oxford University Press, 2003.

[2] Maleska, Eugene T. *Crosstalk*. Simon & Schuster, 1993, p. 28.

[3] *The New York Times*, April 18, 2003, p. F3.

[4] *The New Yorker*, "The Cartoon Issue," November 17, 2003, pp. 136–137.

[5] *The New York Times*, August 1, 2004, p. 9.

[6] Alcott, Anne. *Math Crossword Puzzles*. 1st Books, 2004.

[7] See "Cryptic," p. 38.

Brain Food

Before we get to the dessert, the "FUN" portion, let's spoon up the entrée—the "FOOD" part.

Though the medical and science people continue to report in qualmish, guarded, scrupulously precise, diffident terms, reading between the lines, any perceptive reader will discover that the research teams are having difficulty containing their enthusiasm. Their findings all indicate that crossword puzzling, among other "cognitively stimulating activities," rewards seniors with not only an enhancement of the quality of their lives, but may also help to ward off Alzheimer's disease, AD in medical shorthand. Numbers of clinical and field studies over the last decade seem to provide convincing evidence of that conclusion. Scores of such reports appear on the Internet, most supported by reference to articles published in respected medical journals.

However, if the Internet is suspect in your view, fifty-two such studies are noted in the *Journal of the American Medical Association (JAMA)* article, "Participation in Cognitively Stimulating Activities and Risk of Incident Alzheimer's Disease."[1] A second study which attracted media attention across the country (newspapers, radio, television) appeared in the *New England Journal of Medicine (NEJOM)*, "Leisure Activities and the Risk of Dementia in the Elderly."[2] It lists forty-two citations. Finally, in this matter of numbers, a brief computer review of recent articles akin to the *JAMA* report

above, threw up twelve pages of such reports, one hundred and three articles.

Enough about numbers. The *NEJOM* test, started in 1980 at the Albert Einstein College of Medicine in the Bronx, New York, tracked 469 seniors over age 75, reporting on the nature and extent of their leisure activities including board games, dancing, music (playing, not listening) and crosswords. The findings bolstered the evidence shown in previous studies— that exercising the mind through participation in board games, chess, bridge, continuing education, and crosswords helps to provide potent protection against Alzheimer's Disease or other forms of mental deterioration. The seniors who engaged in such pastimes lowered the risk of AD by up to 75% as compared to non-participants.

Joe Verghese, lead author of the *NEJOM* story, wrote that activities such as chess, board games, violin playing, and bridge seemed to have a greater effect than crosswords—a result not found in other reports, but he also noted that frequency of participation was an important factor. So, one may reasonably ask, "how many quintagenarians, sexagenarians, or septuagenarians would take up the fiddle?" Ballroom dancing, the only physical activity that showed positive results, is normally a once-a month, or at best, a once-a-week program for any such involved senior.

Board games all require a competing partner or partners, a

serious limitation on frequency. Crosswords, however, may be enjoyed any time, all the time: at meals, in bed, on the toilet and bath, in restaurants, on the road, in hotels, in hospitals, at the dentist, waiting in ticket lines, in lengthy road delays, waiting for the spouse to show, on backpack or camping trips, waiting for planes, trains, or ferries, aboard a plane, train, or ferry, etc. (all examples taken from personal experience as you may have gathered). A cruciverbal enthusiast could solve thirty or forty crosswords between dance sessions and a dozen or more grids while waiting for the Yahtzee or Backgammon opponent to show. And crosswords are cheap; they come with the daily newspaper or in inexpensive book form.

As to probable frequency of participation, none of the other activities studied can come within a mile of crosswords. Actually, only one other leisure activity, reading, can match crosswords, and reading, the greatest of all leisure activities, does not seem to stretch the mind adequately.

A news release from the National Institute of Health[3] underscores that very point. Commenting on the *JAMA* study noted above, the Institute wrote that "In comparing the levels of cognitive activity with diagnoses of AD, the researchers found that the frequency of activity was related to the risk of developing AD. For each point increase of frequency on the participant's scores on the scale of cognitive activities, the risk of developing AD decreased by 33 percent. On average, compared with someone with the lowest activity level, the risk was reduced by 47 percent among those whose frequency of activity was highest (p. 21)."

The release also stated, "This study provides important new evidence that there may be something to the notion of increased cognitive activity and reduced risk of Alzheimer's Disease. Further research should help better to sort out whether cognitive activities can be prescribed to reduce risk of AD and why that may be so (p.1)." As a sidebar, that last caveat is lost on the entrepreneurs who have followed where science has led, for currently the book market holds more than a dozen works on how to exercise the mind. None of these volumes deal with warding off Alzheimer's Disease, that subject might not sell, but rather how to develop Einsteinian mind muscles or how to raise your IQ. Such is the stuff of such publications as *Building Mental Muscle* (David Gammon and Allen D. Bragdon), and *Brain Builders Lifelong Guide* (Richard Leviton), and *The Einstein Factor* (Win Wenger and Richard Poe). Several of these kinds of works, such as *Brain Building Games* (Allen Bragdon and David Gammon), trumpet "3 MONTHS TO A BETTER BRAIN: 176 Performance Tips…To Increase Memory, Math, and Language Skills," and "A 90-day mental exercise program."

Laughable! But hold on. Two highly regarded medical research specialists, Guy McKhann of Harvard and Johns Hopkins and Marilyn Albert, director of the Gerontology Research Unit at Massachusetts General Hospital, conducted a ten-year study of 3,000 seniors, starting in 1985. In mid-2003 they published the results in *Keep Your Brain Young* (Wiley, New York). They, too, recommend a set regimen of regular physical exercise, maintenance of a positive personal attitude which includes regular sleep patterns, stress avoidance, continued sexual activity, and moderate alcohol tippling, along with reading, bridge games, attendance at lectures, and, very important, working crosswords. Not only will your brain function more efficiently, say the authors, but you will also live longer.

Joseph T. Coyle of the Harvard Medical School, Department of Psychiatry, sums it up in "Use It or Lose It—Do Effortful Mental Activities Protect Against Dementia,"[4] "The persistent engagement of the elderly in effortful mental activities may promote plastic changes in the brain that circumvent the pathology underlying the symptoms of dementia… In the meantime, seniors should be encouraged to read, play board games, and go ballroom dancing" and, we add very strongly, do crosswords, "because these activities at the very least enhance their quality of life and they just might do more than that."

[1] February 13, 2002, pp. 742–748.

[2] June 19, 2003, pp. 2508–2516.

[3] *NIH News Release*, "National Institute on Aging," Tuesday, February 2, 2002.

[4] *New England Journal of Medicine*, June 19, 2003, pp. 2489–2490.

Crosswords & Alzheimer's

Reading newspapers or books, playing games like cards or checkers, doing crosswords or other puzzles, going to museums, watching television, or listening to the radio—those and other activities that "stimulate" the mind may cut the risk of Alzheimer's disease.

Researchers asked more than 800 Alzheimer's-free people aged 65 or older how often they participated in mentally challenging activities. Four years later, the people who had reported more mental activity were less likely to have the disease. Physical activity had no impact on risk.

What to do: This study doesn't *prove* that crossword puzzles will ward off Alzheimer's disease. If Alzheimer's starts ten years before it's diagnosed, it's possible that the people who didn't read, do puzzles, etc., already had an early form of the disease that was too mild for the researchers to detect when the study began. But it doesn't hurt to keep your mind moving.

Neurology 59: 1910, 2002.

The Real Crosswordese

Like many another vocation and avocation, crosswords has developed a lingo of its own. Herewith, the terms every cruciverbalist should know.

Across: The first of a pair of words which form the most widely used term in crosswords. The second word is, of course, "down." Across pertains to the entries running from left to right on the grid. Down refers to those entries running top to bottom. The term "across and down" is so broadly understood, it may serve as a synonym for crosswords.

Cheater: Any black square that does not divide a long white slot into two slots (as a black square in a corner or on the edge of the grid).

Check: A term in American crosswords to indicate that a letter appears in an across word and a down word. In American crosswords every letter

The Vermont Country Store®
Purveyors of the Practical & Hard-To-Find

Winter Comforts

Across
1. Snow tires for shoes p.42
5. Our home town p.2
6. Plug-in blanket p.3
9. Sheep_____ ear warmers p.36
11. Wilbur_____ p.88
12. Boysenberry, peach, plum p.82
14. Instant heat in a jar p.119
15. Hot_____ bottle p.119

Down
2. Pronounced "chow-da" p.89
3. Dirt grabbers p.74, 31
4. PJs, downhill, or X-country p.66
7. Easy opener, p.81
8. Keeps drinks hot p.81
10. Thinskins, longjohns p.59, 60-62
13. Proprietor p.2

Voice of the Mountains
Winter 2004
The Orton Family Business Since 1946
WESTON, VERMONT
www.**vermontcountrystore**.com

must appear in two words. Unchecked squares are verboten. A synonym for Key.

Clue: The word(s) or phrase the constructor provides seeking the answer. The question. The definition. ✱

Clue Tag: *See* Tag.

Constructor: The title in the United States for creators of American crosswords.

Cover: A term used here to indicate a letter abutted by a black or filled white square. Thus, uncovered means a letter with an adjoining open white square.

Crosswordese: Answers that appear repeatedly. However, to Scalawaggers, crosswordese is the unusual, bizarre, freaky answer to which the perplexed constructor sometimes resorts.

Cruciverb: Synonym for crossword. Factitious word derived from a conflation of the Latin for cross and word. Factitious, yes, but widely accepted in the crossword community. (Google shows 21,700 entries for the word cruciverb.) Thus, cruciverbalist = crossword person, cruciverbing = doing crosswords, etc.

Cryptic: The title applied to the crossword puzzle form popular throughout England. Also known as the English crossword.

Definition: Synonym for clue, but clue is preferred.

Down: *See* Across.

Editor: The crossword adept who amends and certifies the constructors' grids and prepares the puzzles for publication. Often a constructor as well.

English Crossword: *See* Cryptic.

Entry: The answer to the clue.

Fill: All the non-theme entries.

Grid: The puzzle seen as an entity. A synonym for crossword. Grid is always used to describe the puzzle size: 15 x 15 grid, 21 x 21 grid, etc.

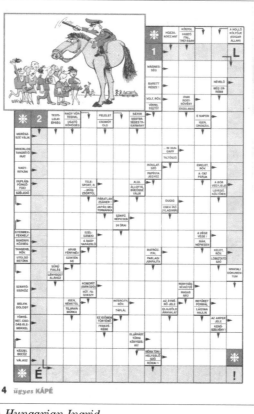

A Hungarian Ingrid

Ingrid: A nickname scalawaggers apply to the "clue in grid" form of crossword favored by many European cruciverbalists. According to Will Shortz, the French call them arrow words, "But in most countries they're known as Scandinavian-style crosswords (or some variation on that), because the format originated in Denmark and then the rest of Scandinavia."

Key: A synonym for check. A term in American crosswords to indicate that a letter appears in an across word and a down word. In American crosswords, every letter must appear in two words. Unkeyed squares are verboten.

Light: In cryptic crosswords, the answer to the clue, cryptic crossword synonym for the American term, "entry."

Pattern: The design of the crossword. The placement of the black squares on the grid.

Repeaters: Entries that keep appearing over and over again.

Setter: The title in England for creators of English cryptic crosswords.

Size: The number of black and white squares across the grid. Since the grid is symmetric, the number down the grid will be the same as across. All grids are odd numbered in size, running 13 x 13 (small) to 23 x 23 (Sunday sized), but usually 15 x 15 to 21 x 21.

Slot: The set of squares that accommodates the entry.[1]

Solution: The answer to the clue. *See* entry.

Solver: That's you, the riddle person.

Square: The American grid is composed of white and black squares.

Stack: Three or more across entries of the same length arranged one atop the other. In down, three or more entries, arranged side by side.

Symmetry: A requirement of American puzzles. The pattern must be identical upside down as it is right side up.

Tag: An indicator provided by the constructor to express a modification of the clue. Also called a clue tag.

A Norwegian Ingrid

Theme: The puzzle motif. A characteristic common to several entries.

✱ Clue: By convention the clue is a compressed, terse, bare bones locution which the solver must subconsciously expand to a full clarifying sentence or phrase in order to discover the entry. Even the simplest clues require this mental leap:

> Bloomer et al = Give Bloomer's other name(s) and make it plural

> Big _____ conference = There is an organization, probably athletic, called the Big something conference. What is that something?

Many clues require greater consideration:

> Hush-hush D.C. org = Provide the abbreviated name for a national governmental organization or agency that operates in secret.

> A little of this, a little of that = What word means composed of bits and pieces.

Portrayal in "They Died With Their Boots On" = A movie or a play called, "They Died With Their Boots On" includes a particular role. Name that role.

Moves like a leveret = What is a leveret and how does it move?

If solvers cannot make that mental transition to an explicatory expression, they should realize that they are dealing with a difficult hidden definition.

---

[1] Thanks to Patrick Berry.

Rules of the Game

A major edition of Hoyle's[1] lists the rules for more than 500 games but, astoundingly, there is not a single rule for the crosswords game that is ten to one hundred times more popular than the amusements listed in that edition. Again, my favorite edition of Roget[2] lists under "Sports and Games" the names of 174 games, and again crosswords is conspicuously absent. Apparently, these works assume that crosswords exists sans regulation, and is, therefore, not a game. They are wrong on both counts.

From the beginning, crossword editors have insisted on certain principles, which over the years have hardened into dictates. These are the overt rules for constructors, available from the crossword editors of *The New York Times*, *The Los Angeles Times*, *The Washington Post*, or your favorite newspaper.

In summary, all American editors require:

1. No two-letter entries. Minimum word length is three letters. Thus, the popular clue "Hesitation sounds" always appears in the plural (Ers and Ums), as does "Sounds of inquiry"(Ehs).

2. The grid pattern must be symmetrical. If turned upside down, the puzzle must look exactly as it did upside-up. (That rule is emphasized by an exceptional exception. A *New York Times* puzzle, No. 0603, constructed by a confirmed "contrarian," declared itself deliberately "asymmetric" in conformance with its theme that "conventionality is not morality.")[3]

3. Every letter must be keyed. That is, each letter must appear in both an across and a down word.

4. Answers must not be repeated on the grid.

5. The black squares must not isolate a white area. The grid must interlock overall.

6. Long (theme) entries must be placed symmetrically on the grid.

7. The black squares must be limited (informally, less than 16%), and black squares should not clump or cluster on the grid.

8. Invented words are verboten. Each word should have a printed reference or be a part of current speech.

9. The answer must not repeat a word used in the clue.

In addition to the rules, editors recommend the use of everyday speech, the inclusion of wit and humor, entries with the lesser used letters J, K, Q, W, X, Z, and the avoidance of words beginning with RE, or IN, plurals, third person singulars, or past tense (too easy).

Knowledge of these rules may help solvers indirectly, but of direct applicability is the unwritten and somewhat recondite principle, the rule of agreement. The rule of agreement is of the greatest consequence for solvers, for it holds over a variety of clue types and probably accounts for the majority of answers by rule. The prescript stipulates that the answer must correspond or agree with the clue. Simply, if the clue is singular, the answer must be singular, if plural, then plural:

Welles = Orson

Welles or Bean = Orson

Welles and Bean = Orsons

Hyson = Tea

Hyson or Pekoe = Tea

Hyson and Pekoe = Teas

Turkeys = Toms

Octavia's lips = Labia

If the clue holds an abbreviation, the answer will be abbreviated:

Rambler mfr. = AMC

NYC subways = IRT and BMT

Lyricist's org. = ASCAP

MTV watchers = Teens

JFK's VP = LBJ

Util. output = Elec.

Role for Liz = Cleo

Some abbreviations which have become standard terms in our speech, such as inc, amp, and math, may not call for an abbreviation, but double check to be sure.

If the clue is in the present tense, likewise the answer, and if in the past tense—then past tense:

Inflict = Wreak

Inflicted = Wreaked

Help = Support

Helped = Supported

Similar agreement holds for the grammatical forms of "person:"

(I understood) Sniggle = Eel

(He understood) Sniggles = Eels

Give = Donate

Gives = Donates

Hum = Drone

Hums = Drones

Overall, if the clue is adjectival, the answer must be an adjective; an adverb calls for an adverb, verb for verb, noun for noun, etc.:

More unctuous = Oilier

Please speak = Quietly

Contaminate = Taint

Handles clumsily = Paws

City on the Thames = Henley

To put it simply and grammatically, the answer must agree with the clue as a part of speech. Of the eight parts of speech: adjectives, adverbs, nouns, pronouns, and verbs are common answers, while prepositions, conjunctions, and interjections are rare visitors. Beyond such grammatical agreements are other correspondences. If the first name is used in the clue it calls for a first name, last name then last name:

Clark's co-star in "It Happened One Night" = Claudette

Gable's co-star in "It Happened One Night" = Colbert

Farah and Jaclyn's co-star = Kate

Roosevelt's VEEP: 1933 = Garner

Adolf's mistress = Eva

If neither name is used, the answer should be the last name:

Thirty-ninth president = Carter

He supposedly introduced pasta to Italy = Polo

In the rare instance when a comic or fictional character is known exclusively or chiefly by a first name then, of course, the first name holds:

Sgt. Snorkel's canine companion = Otto

That pink sock loving kitty = Mooch

The meanest cat in comicsville = Bucky

A foreign name or word requires a corresponding answer:

The head of Pierre = Tete

Bodies of eau = Mers

Hans' expression of dismay = Ach

Kind of hosen = Leder

_____ Sprach Zarathustra = Also

Poivre's partner = Sel

Oktoberfest sales = Biers

Fuel for lorries = Petrol

_____ favor amigo = Por

Agreement is particularly important for geographical, regional, and national clues:

City of northwest Italy = Turin

City of northwest Italia = Torino

City north of Genoa = Milan

City north of Genova = Milano

If the area in the clue is spelled the same in English as in the foreign tongue, be prepared for either possibility:

City north of Siena = Firenze or Florence

Of course, if the clue is in a foreign language, the answer will follow in that language:

La plume de ma _____ = Tante

Heilige nacht = Weihnachten

On occasion the language may be hidden:

Always at the forum = Semper

Life in Paris = La vie

Other such required agreements appear frequently in current crosswords and new ones are waiting to be invented. As puzzles grow more tricky, the agreement elements become ever more subtle. Solvers must be on the alert or, as Gigi might say, "Qui vive."

[1] Frey, Richard L. *The New Complete Hoyle.* Doubleday, 1991.

[2] *Roget's International Thesaurus.* 3rd ed. Crowell, 1962.

[3] *New York Times*, #0603, 2004.

ACROSS

1 Often-told truths
5 ___ facto
9 Tricky shot
14 Racer Luyendyk
15 Gardener's purchase
16 Some saxes
17 Lava geese
18 It's passed on
19 Contents of some John Cage compositions
20 Start of a question
23 Adjusts
24 Big ___
25 Whomps, briefly
28 Old Mideast combine: Abbr.
29 John Dean, to Nixon
32 Sure way to lose money
34 "Gosh!"
35 Ruined
37 A star may have one
38 Middle of the question
41 Place
43 Discernment
44 Common ratio
46 Sample
50 Chamber piece?
49 Dispatched
51 Monk's title
52 Driver's aid: Abbr.
54 Track racer
56 End of the question
60 Like workhorses
62 Arcade name
63 V.I.P.'s opposite
64 It's passed on
65 Compelled
66 Wading bird
67 Ottawa-born singer/songwriter
68 Turned up
69 Cry that might be appropriate at this point in the puzzle

ACROSS

1 Retreat
2 Passage between buildings
3 Bingo announcement
4 "Toodles!"
5 Mirage
6 Magician's sound effect
7 Draped dress
8 Things to be read
9 Om, e.g.
10 Cream ingredient
11 Malodorous pest
12 Coded message
13 Language suffix often seen in crosswords
13 Compass dir. often seen in crosswords
21 African grazer
22 Put words in someone's mouth?
26 Anthem contraction
27 Platform place: Abbr.
30 Is hip to
31 1995 country hit "Someone ___ Star"
33 "Dagnabbit!"
35 Latched
36 Affectedly dainty, in England
37 Extinct Namibian shrub genus: Var.
38 Coordinated effort
39 Like some seats
40 First
41 Trip producer
42 W.W. II Pacific battle site, for short
44 Appropriate
45 Blazing
47 Cat
48 Desired response to "Take my wife ... please!"
50 Open-sided shelter
53 Perfume source
55 Noted archer
57 What a germ may become
58 Good sign
59 Ticks off
60 Hearst kidnapping grp.
61 Dear

Puzzle by Patrick Merrell

Editor's note:

Today's puzzle contains 10 deliberate "mistakes" that are part of the puzzle solution.

For answers, call 1-900-285-5656, $1.20 a minute; or, with a credit card, 1-800-814-5554.

Annual subscriptions are available for the best of Sunday crosswords from the last 50 years: 1-888-7-ACROSS.

Editor's note: Today's puzzle contains 10 deliberate "mistakes" that are part of the puzzle solution.

Smart Start—Pattern Wise

You start a crossword by starting! That's it. You may if you wish start at the bottom right and work your way up—but why? There may not be a correct method, but there is a sensible way—start at 1-Across, and go on from there. That mode has at least two virtues: we are accustomed to reading across rather than down, and it is easier to follow one's progress if we trot numerically through the grid. Some crossword adepts recommend a quick run through the entire grid filling in the easy clues: missing words, names, and short entries. That strategy is okay if, contrary to their advice, you also fill in the plural "s," the third person,

present tense "s," the past tense "ed," and some of the other starting tips you will discover in SCALAWAG. However, you will achieve the same results working systematically across and down, so do what pleases you best. A companion tip recommends working all around a completed entry to find as many crossing words as possible. Good advice in any system.

Having started at 1-Across, there are many ways to proceed, but one best way. Some crossword masochists, who find most puzzles too simple for their efforts, do only the "Down" clues to complete their grids. Some day you may be among that group, but for starters, don't even think about it. Most puzzlers try to complete the block at the upper left before moving on, but one caveat. Either by happenstance or deliberation, that upper block may be, occasionally, the most difficult unit of the puzzle. **Tip:** move on to the next logical block. It is surprising how easily the answers may come once some intervening letters make an appearance. That next logical block is determined, almost always, by the grid pattern; the pattern will specify your next step and the consequent pathway to the solution. Hence, a major SCALAWAG tenet: the pattern provides the best procedural guide; follow it.

There are as many patterns as there are constructors, but several general patterns crop up frequently, and the principles involved in filling those patterns may be applied to all crossword grid forms. Using the pattern to govern the fill process will speed you on your way across and down, and lead you to consummation. In the examples which follow, the sequences may vary in relation to the entry hit rate (2 may be filled in before 1, or 3 before 2, etc.), but always let your pattern be your guide.

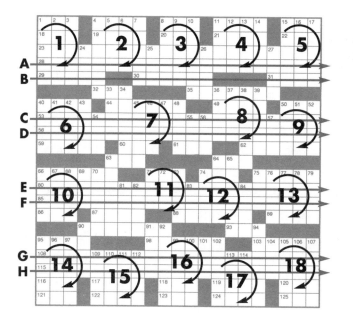

1. The straight across the grid pattern is particularly effective when the clue, almost always a theme clue, calls for an entry that runs all across or almost all across the grid: lengthy quotations or lines of poetry (usual doggerel).

2. Very popular is the diagonal-oriented grid, sometimes so heavily structured that its pattern screams, "Solve me this way!"

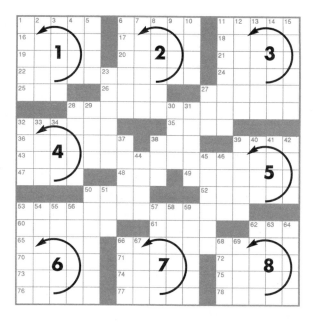

3. The block-by-block design is a recurrent form, with discrete units connected to other units of the grid as required by the rules but separated only as far as the editors permit.

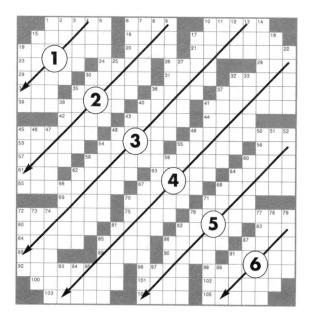

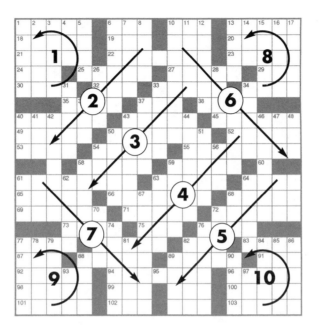

4. A grid combining forms 2 and 3 is a popular design.

6. The anyway you want to do it pattern makes an appearance at times. Have fun.

5. The diamond pattern is handsome, eye-catching, and is best approached with a specific plan of attack.

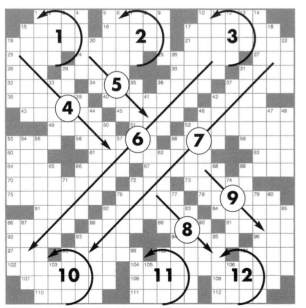

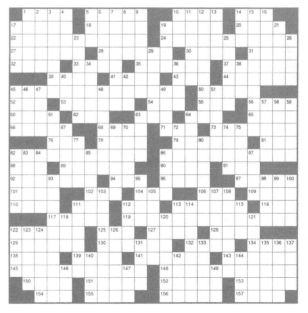

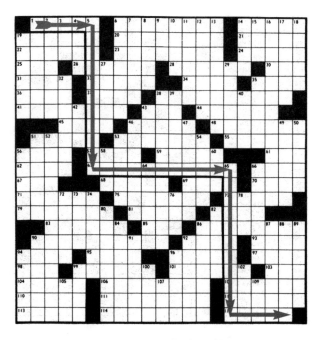

7. Since Maleska's death, I have seen just one new "Stepquote," a quotation which drops in steps from upper left to bottom right. However, if you run into an oldie, try filling in the crossing letters until you can make a stab at the quote.

Themes

A theme is a characteristic; it may be anything under the sun, common to a number of entries in a crossword. It is perhaps best understood as the motif of the puzzle. Many puzzles have titles illustrative of the theme: "By George" contains a lengthy quotation by G.B.S. In "Double Cross," two similar letters occupy a single white square in more than a dozen entries. "Pun Fun" is packed with word play. "Galaxy" has the word "star" occupying a single square thirteen times. "Under Canvas" shows a group of entries regarding the circus. And, "As Romans Did" uses Roman numerals throughout the grid.

Although some few puzzlers dislike themes—heck, there are even some earthlings averse to chocolate—most riddlers find that themes add fun, spice, and occasional awe to the riddling process. Themes may not have rules as strict as those for the crossword itself, but over time the principles guiding themes have almost hardened into semi-rules. The difference between rule and principle: on occasion and only for good reason, the principle may be broken.

Principle 1

A minimum of three entries should be theme oriented, but three is skimpy and disappointing. Good puzzles show at least four or five theme answers, and sometimes more than a dozen.

Principle 2

Generally, theme answers should be the longest entries in the grid. This principle may be broken to accommodate a multiplicity (seven or more) of short entries.

Principle 3

Theme entries should be arranged symmetrically on the grid. Again, this rule applies to only the three, four, or five lengthy answers, and not to the theme of many short entries.

Principle 4

Theme entries, particularly poetry, doggerel, and quotations should run across the grid rather than down. Again, the short responses are excepted.

Principle 5

Theme entries should look and be grammatically consistent. They should be of the same part of speech and about the same length.

Simple themes have been around almost as long as crosswords themselves and continue to this day. Such themes may explain some of the disfavor, because they are too easy and may become tedious. A dairy theme I encountered had the word "butter" as a repetitive word. Any time a "U" or a "T" appeared in a six letter word, it was a signal to enter the word butter, and it always worked. Other simple themes fill the grid with lesser used letters like "K" in Kankakee, Kafka, khaki, kiosk, and kinky; "W" in wow, werewolf, whew, and who's who; or "Q" in Albuquerque, quinquagesima, and risqué. "S" is also popular as a theme letter and one puzzle filled the grid with esses, and a track of those esses revealed a giant "S" occupying the center of the grid. Another "S" theme labeled "PSSST" showed three esses in a row by combining a two-word answer:

Phrase in many dietary foods = Lesssalt

It has 32 men = Chessset

Other simple themes call for former presidents: Polk, Taft, Bush, and Ford. Or colorful regions: Blue Nile, Greenland, Red Bank, Orange, and Asheville. Or a substitution of Latin for English:

Frank Sinatra = Olblueoculi

Bond foe = Aurumfinger

Insincere show of sorrow = Crocodile lacrimae

However, there are hundreds of ingenious themes that add amusement and instruction to their grids. Puzzlers are familiar with doggerel which wends its rhythmic way across four full lines of a grid, or a lengthy quotation which also provides the author and the source of the quote, or Maleska's "Stepquote," a quotation which drops in steps from upper left to bottom right.

As noted above, a popular theme device requires two letters or an entire word crammed into a single square, or the opposite approach, which calls for the elimination of a letter or an entire word from the answer. A bodacious "Golf" puzzle placed the form "one" as part of a longer word immediately under the form "par," also part of a longer word:

ComPARe

AtONEd

APARtment

LONEsome

Thus, in six instances the puzzle read "one under par." Ingenious—what! A similar cunningly designed puzzle showed "one on one" a half dozen times.

BONE

MONEy

Still another surprisingly inventive theme required riddlers to read the clue backwards and forwards and to provide an answer that read both ways as well:

Spacer = Stenosbarserit

Devil = Evilonetlewd

Stressed = Accentedseip

Word play (such as homophones, Spoonerisms, Tom Swifties, malapropisms, anagrams, riddles, and puns) is meat for the themer:

Texas trial = Laredo ordeal (anagram)

Philippines beast = Manila animal (anagram)

Odd magazine = Harper's Bizarre (pun)

Chemical flower = Oxide daisy (pun)

Why is Y like a romance novel = It ends happily (Riddle)

Tundra hairdresser = Styling moose (Homophone)

Instant coffee said Tom_____ = Groundlessly (Swiftie)

It adds up said Tom _____ = Summarily (Swiftie)

Mr. Malaprop's inflamed throat = Sore phalanx

Mr. M's words for the New York Subway = Mash transit

A hundred newly minted word games invented by ingenious

constructors appear annually, such as the puzzle labeled "Fractured Polysyllables," which required the solver to interpret each syllable of a polysyllabic word:

> Opposed to a banner share = Conflagration
>
> Deduce a refusal = Inferno
>
> Contract debt chits = Incurious
>
> Panning the cold cuts shops = Deliberating
>
> Svelte monarch = Thinking

On occasion, an abstruse theme is uncovered only after the constructor provides the key. At first, the answers seem to make no sense:

> Franklin D. Roosevelt museum site = Warm mans Georgia
>
> T. Williams play = Suddenly last man

Until the constructor provides the key:

> Film or play that is the key to the puzzle = A man for all seasons

Thus, substituting the appropriate season for the word "man" solved the conundrum:

> Franklin D. Roosevelt museum site = Warm Springs Georgia
>
> T. Williams play = Suddenly last summer

In another across and downer a half dozen entries seemed meaningless until the missing theme key, "Get lost," was entered on the grid. Following normal curciverb hint-play, the word "get" was then applied to the nonsensical six, and the problem popped:

> "Understand?" = (Get) The message
>
> Be a hindrance = (Get) In one's way.

There are scores of other theme types, seemingly too numerous and too irregular to classify, but Patrick Berry takes a stab at the chore and comes up with about twenty categories[1]. In general, cracking the theme is a giant step toward cracking the puzzle. **Tip:** If the puzzle is titled, that title is your best hint to the theme. Scalawaggers must develop theme awareness antennae. Start now!

---

[1] Berry, Patrick, *Crossword Challenges for Dummies*. Wiley Publishing Inc., 2004, pp. 82–90.

Pen or Pencil: Obs.

From the beginning of crosswords, solvers were confronted by the phrase, "Pen or Pencil," a seemingly innocuous phrase that has occasioned considerably more heat than light, more incitement than insight, more sins than sense. "Pencil" is the stand-in term for those who believe it is sound and productive to fill in possible answers while working down the grid, even if those answers are somewhat shaky, and later to erase if the crossing words prove the initial answer to be incorrect. "Pen" stands for those crosswarders who balk at filling in the white squares until the answer is verified, the choice confirmed. Those veteran solvers have

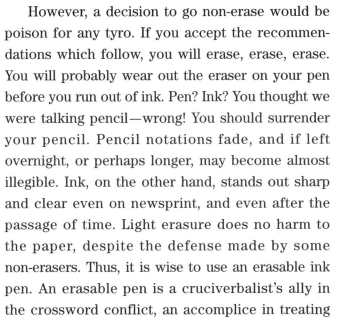

been described as egomaniacs, grandstanders, or show-offs, but who's to judge? Whether the motive is ego or affectation is immaterial, for crosswords are designed for sport, entertainment, and enlightenment. If experts get their kicks from a "no erasure" system, so be it: one man's potion is another man's poison.

However, a decision to go non-erase would be poison for any tyro. If you accept the recommendations which follow, you will erase, erase, erase. You will probably wear out the eraser on your pen before you run out of ink. Pen? Ink? You thought we were talking pencil—wrong! You should surrender your pencil. Pencil notations fade, and if left overnight, or perhaps longer, may become almost illegible. Ink, on the other hand, stands out sharp and clear even on newsprint, and even after the passage of time. Light erasure does no harm to the paper, despite the defense made by some non-erasers. Thus, it is wise to use an erasable ink pen. An erasable pen is a cruciverbalist's ally in the crossword conflict, an accomplice in treating trickery, and an accessory before and after the commitment to fill the white squares. It is a decades-old invention which seems to have been devised with crosswarders in mind, and should be recorded as a major advance in the history of crosswords.

Thus, "Pen or Pencil" is now obsolete—we should all be "Pens."

Look It Up—Write It Down

Even more vociferous than the "non-erasers" is the "no reference book" crowd. They have elevated puzzle solving sans references to the level of a moral crusade. Using a dictionary or an encyclopedia is cheating and a heinous sin, they maintain. This crew declares that the use of a reference work displays a lack of personal integrity and is a sign of a feckless, glaikit, vacuous, solver. Again, why argue. How solvers find gratification in crosswords is personal, unique, sui genesis. There is a third camp, however, midway between the two extremes, which argues that the use of two or three readily at hand references is not only acceptable but advisable and assists in the flow of the game, but that frequent and/or long interruptions to find guidance does dull the sport. Personally, I fall into that third camp. I restrict myself to two reference works for most puzzles, an excellent desk dictionary and a good crossword dictionary. For difficult puzzles, I will get out of bed or off my duff to consult a variety of sources, but I will never, never use the computer. Unreasonable! Inconsistent! Yes, but I toss back Emerson's old chestnut, "A foolish consistency is the hobgoblin of little minds."

Further, on the controversy, constructors and editors from Margaret Farrar on knew that the use of reference works would add to one's store of words[1] and open worlds of knowledge and gratification for solvers:

Who was Creusa and who/what did she abandon?

Is it true what they say about Dixie?

Cyaxares was a what?

Yegg, what a peculiar word, what is its origin?

Is threnody an antonym of elegy?

Miriam is punished for what transgression?

What is so strange about Amalthea's horn?

What is the plural of moose?

What/who is Cawdor?

Tignish lies where, and why is the location abbreviated?

Did Virgil write "amor vincit ommia," or was it an Englishman?

Did the Bard write "all that glitters is not gold" or "nor all that glisters, gold."

English includes scores of Latin words and phrases: What is the meaning of

    ne plus ultra

    ipse dixit

    Deo volente

    caveat emptor

    magna cum laude

    ora pro nobis

Several thousand such questions have been answered by my reference books, accumulated in part from the days when I taught "Reference" at The Columbia University School of Library Service, and increased by purchases at thrift shops, garage sales, and library over-stock sell-outs. Of course, such purchases are practical only for those works not obsolesced by date.

Constructors, necessarily, develop reference libraries and some accounts indicate that such libraries may run to scores, if not hundreds, of titles. Maleska wrote that he developed his collection by requesting friends and family to present particular reference works in lieu of "clothes or gadgets or other presents on my birthday or at Christmas."[2] He mentions specific titles and a large list of subject areas in his collection. He notes his distaste for crossword dictionaries and answers provided by telephone call, but then writes, "if solvers consult reference books to find answers to clues in puzzles, they are not cheating. After all, the constructors and editors resort to such books regularly."[3] Apparently, finding the answer in a reference work is right and proper, but crossword dictionar-

BREWER'S DICTIONARY OF PHRASE AND FABLE

GIVING ILLUSTRATIVE QUOTATIONS FROM THE WORKS OF THE MOST FAMOUS AUTHORS FROM THE EARLIEST TIMES DOWN TO THE PRESENT DAY; A HISTORY OF THE CHIEF FIGURES MENTIONED IN THE MYTHOLOGIES OF THE WORLD; A RECORD OF SUPERSTITIONS AND CUSTOMS, ANCIENT AND MODERN; AN EXPLANATION OF PHRASES COMMONLY IN USE IN THE ENGLISH LANGUAGE, OF NATIVE ORIGIN OR BORROWED FROM OTHER TONGUES; ANCIENT CANT AND MODERN SLANG, WITH THEIR EQUIVALENTS IN OTHER LANGUAGES OF EUROPE; THE STORIES OF WELL-KNOWN CHARACTERS FROM NOVELS AND ROMANCES; LOCAL AND NATIONAL LEGENDS; A GLOSSARY OF SCIENTIFIC, HISTORICAL, POLITICAL, AND ARCHÆOLOGICAL TERMS AND EVENTS; REFERENCES BEARING ON EVERY DESCRIPTION OF ECONOMIC AND SCIENTIFIC DATA; ETYMOLOGICAL AND MUCH OTHER MISCELLANEOUS INFORMATION.

BY THE
Rev. E. COBHAM BREWER, LL.D.

NEW EDITION
Thoroughly Revised

PHILADELPHIA
J. B. LIPPINCOTT COMPANY
1931

ies and phone answers are N.G. to Maleska.

Despite Maleska's dictum, a good crossword dictionary is the second book I would recommend for any novice crossworder. These dictionaries are designed to provide lists of synonyms, near synonyms, and closely associated words for the thousands of key words the dictionary editors select as likely to appear in cross-words; sometimes more than two pages of such synonyms but usually five to twenty possibles are arranged by word length and then by alphabet:

FLORID = fine, high, buxom, fresh, ruddy, ornate, rococo, rubied, asiatic, flowery, taffeta, blooming, figurative, rubicund, sanguine, splendid, vigorous.

RHYTHMIC = poetic, pulsing, regular, cadenced, measured, metrical, cadential, pulsating.

These citations attest to a glory of the English language, its phenomenal vocabulary. That extraordinary word list is a testament to our language's ability and willingness to absorb words from other languages and weave them seamlessly into our tongue. B.J. Holmes notes that English holds 49 "words we can use to describe a friend."[4] Ludicrously and amazingly, but also authoritatively, Kate Burridge, Australia's preeminent lexicologist, writes, "Over the years English has also accumulated more than 2,500 expressions for male and female genitalia."[5]

There are more than a score of such dictionaries on store shelves, each one proclaiming its superiority: "world's best puzzle finisher," "newest, most comprehensive and authoritative," "world's best selling," "America's foremost," "most comprehensive," "most complete," "the ultimate reference," etc., etc. I like six really good ones: *The New York Times*, Swanfeldt's,[6] *The New Comprehensive A–Z, Webster's New World, The Random House, Simon & Schuster's Super*. Each of these six offers some unique special features: ease of use, a separate reference section, special tables, a mini atlas, particular sections on popular crossword subjects such as : Shakespeare, sports, mythology, or the Bible. And they are all chock-a-block with words. One dictionary notes current "synonyms for more than 200,000 words," another, "more than 300,000 clues and answer words," and still another declares, "more than 700,000 clues and answer words," and now *The Million Word Crossword Dictionary*. Check for yourself. You can hardly go wrong among the top half dozen. However, one caveat: most of these dictionaries come in two sizes: a large size occasionally available in hard cover, and a small size. As the size gets smaller so does the type face. Take heed not only of your pocket book but also of your eyesight. A useful variant of the crossword dictionary is the crossword key such as *Webster's*

New World Easy Crossword Key which sorts under the full clue rather than the key word and provides a single answer (occasionally two or three):

Important intersection = Crossroads
Cheese city = Edam
Enterprising seafarers of old = Privateers
Haha, e.g. = Fence
Sound of speed in the comics = Voom
Hindu deity = Deva, Kama, Rama, Siva

The top recommendation is, of course, an excellent desk dictionary. Before we get to a particular title, however, a cautionary note applies for all the reference works to follow. The book must be easy to manipulate at the desk or in bed (my frequent solving site). Thus, only single volume works will be noted and they must weigh in under five pounds. If you own a multi-volume encyclopedia, an unabridged dictionary, or an elephant folio atlas—great! But they will not be recommended here for purchase. Secondly, my recommendations are more than merely opinionated, they are downright prejudiced. For every title to be mentioned, there are probably three or four others just as good. If you want objective advice, consult the best, your local public librarian.

I started with the *Webster's Collegiate Dictionary*, fifth edition, 1935 (two pounds, nine ounces), and for most of World War II I carried and still treasure the *Webster's New Handy Dictionary Armed Services Edition*. I moved up to the ninth edition (three pounds, 10 ounces) and then on to the eleventh, 2003 (three pounds, 12 ounces). The *Merriam-Webster's Collegiate Dictionary* also serves as a decent biographical dictionary and gazetteer, and the two score of tables: alphabets, calendars, languages, numbers, weights and measures, and punctuation marks (most very useful for crossword solutions) mark the *Webster's Collegiate*, 11th edition as a great choice for cruciverbalists. Merriam-Webster is a name to be trusted in word books.

That's it for starters. There are several thousand more word and language publications on the market: thesauruses (or thesauri), dictionaries of slang, foreign phrases, word origins, beginnings and endings, idioms and puns, specialized dictionaries for medicine, biology and every other academic discipline. You may want one or two of these volumes as you work your way up to the *New York Times'* Saturday puzzle. Just behind the basic two, some would say it should be the basic three, is the encyclopedia, because a good encyclopedia is a requisite of every literate household. If you don't own a multi-volume encyclopedia, invest in a *Merriam-Webster's Collegiate Encyclopedia*. It's a dandy.

Certain favored subjects crop up frequently in crosswords: the Bible, place names, literary allusions, Shakespeare, major historical figures, language, the classic period, gods and religion, celebrities, and there are a score of books for these such as the *Oxford Essential Guide for Puzzle Solvers* (Berkley Books, 2000) or the "Categories" section of the *New American Crossword Puzzle Dictionary* by Albert Loy, and Philip D. Morehead. (Signet Books, 2004, 3rd ed.) which presume to know what clues will be given and to provide answers in advance to these favorite queries. Their guess is probably better than yours, but you will have more sport finding the answer on your own.

When you are ready to go beyond the basic three, (desk dictionary, crossword dictionary, encyclopedia) the next choice is a toss-up, but I would probably opt for a good world atlas, because all questions such as, "A community on the River Styx" or "A view just east of Eden," require a map. Atlases, however, are subject to P.P.P. (place of publication prejudice). That is, atlases published in England will be heavy on British place names. Similar publications in Italy will generally stress Italian interests and so on. Since we are dealing with American crosswords, it would be wise to acquire an American atlas. Atlas information has been volatile in the last few decades, so be sure to get a current edition. As a rule of thumb, price, map comprehensiveness, and quality seemingly equal, opt for the publication with the most extensive index. Hammond and Rand McNally are respected names in map publication.

One generally assumes a gazetteer should accompany an atlas. True, but be aware that both the desk dictionary and the crossword dictionary are fairly decent as mini gazetteers, and even the atlas index may occasionally serve in that capacity. So, you may be smart to delay such a purchase, but when you decide to go, the *Merriam-Webster's Geographical Dictionary* is a darn good choice.

Biographical queries run through all puzzles, but the solver must distinguish between references for historically important mortals or works dealing with the rage for current pop personality profiles. For the former, there are at least two dozen top bio-dictionaries (including a small section in your desk dictionary), so either toss a coin, or opt for a one-volume Chambers, an old name in this field. Also, since crosswords are rarely interested in the type of reformist corrections that may occur in new editions, a good used volume will probably suffice—and at a significantly lower price.

Language is the blood of crosswords, and English usage hovers over many a crossword clue. Answers galore to such queries are to be found in *The Oxford Companion to the English Language*. The Oxford Companion series is uniformly excellent, and there are dozens of "Companions" on myriad subjects. Three of interest to cruciverbalists are the *Oxford Companion To*: "The Bible," "Philosophy" and "English Literature." Used, older copies of the *Companions* are frequently just right for crossworders.

Literature is a mainstay of constructors, and to go beyond English Lit is the role of *Merriam-Webster's Encyclopedia of Literature*, an unparalleled guide to world literature, authors, terms, and types of all eras. And it just barely slides in under the five pound limit. A top-notch companion to the *Merriam-Webster* is *Benet's Reader's Encyclopedia* by William Rose Benet and Bruce Murphy, now in a revised, updated 4th edition (Harper Collins). Originally, *The Reader's Encyclopedia* by William Rose Benet was the best available and still is useful. The weight limit bans the stellar *Oxford Classical Dictionary*, which weighs in at almost six pounds. Not to fret, the price of the OCD obviously puts it beyond personal reference collections—it's designed for large, well heeled libraries. A couple of golden oldies may take its place: *The Smaller Classical Dictionary* (Everyman) and *Brewer's Dictionary of Phrase and Fable* (Lippincott). Both okay as secondhand purchases.

Frequently overlooked, probably because they are annuals, are the yearly almanacs like *The World Almanac and Book of Facts* and the *Time Almanac*. There is more information crammed between the covers of *The World Almanac* than any other three similarly sized references, and it is particularly useful for cruciverbalists faced with those specifically annoying clues: "Secretary of State under Millard Fillmore," or "Best musical, 1955," or "Baseball rookie of the year, 1982, National," or "Ruler after Edward V." Well, you get the idea. To add to the pleasure, a five-year-old almanac will probably provide 99% of any information required. So pick up a secondhand copy for 25 or 50 cents and never pay the price of the latest edition.

Finally and sadly, our personality and pop culture has invaded crosswords big time. It is a rare puzzle that does not include one or two clues for a pop star, a TV series, a movie title, or a rock/rap entity. When you graduate to the Friday and Saturday *New York Times* puzzles, you may wish to add such references to your library. The market is awash in name finders. Three you will find easy to use are: Coral Amende's *Famous Name Finder*; John C. Plankinton's *Crossword Proper Name Finder*; and Charles D. Edwards' *Crossword Solutions*. Used copies go at a fraction of the original price.

In the movies, if an English language film doesn't appear in either *Video Hound's Golden Movie Retriever* or *Leonard Maltin's Movie and Video Guide*, it was never screened. Both these publications are annuals and a two or three year old edition goes for pennies rather than dollars. Either *Total Television* or *The Complete Directory to Prime Time Networks and Cable TV Shows* are all you will need for the telly. For radio shows, *The Encyclopedia of American Radio* will do the job. These last two are issued serially and an earlier printing will save you mucho dinero.

If you visit any large university library, you will discover more than 100,000 volumes in its "Reference" collection. So be judicious in your acquisitions—you will never get them all. Don't become a reference nut—like me.

[1] Maleska, Eugene T. *A Pleasure in Words*. Simon & Schuster, 1981, pp. 405–412.

[2] Maleska, Eugene T. *Crosstalk*. Simon & Schuster, 1993, pp. 15–16.

[3] Ibid. p.16

[4] Holmes, B.J. *Bradford The Guide to Solving Crosswords: Cracking the Code*. Peter Collin Publishing, 2002, p. 20.

[5] Burridge, Kate. *Blooming English*. Cambridge University Press, 2004, p. 214.

[6] Swanfeldt, Andrew. *Crossword Puzzle Dictionary*. 6th ed. Harper Collins, 1994.

At VI's and VII's—Behind the VIII Ball

Will Weng, the second editor of *The New York Times'* crossword page, reported on a riddle that had stumped him in his salad days:

To double six five hundred add;

'Tis very clear, my little lad.

His sister supplied the answer, "VIVID,"[1] an indication that Roman numbers have long been a staple of riddles. You will discover that every third or fourth puzzle will contain a clue such as, "A year in Trajan's rule," or "The date Ceasar died." However, you will not share Weng's chagrin, for you will know that the constructor is requesting Roman numerals. Constructors love such clues because the crossing words use the numerals as letters. In the two examples given above, you must either know the dates required, hope the crossing words provide the answer, or resort to a reference work on Roman history.

More often, however, the clue when deciphered will disclose a math problem, such as: MCCX + XLV, or MMMX ÷ XXV. For such calculations, the answer is simple, provided you know the Roman numeric table. Hence, a mini-lesson in Roman mathematics (using the mathematical symbols: + = plus or add, - = minus or subtract, x = multiply, and ÷ = divide).

In Roman, the capital letter

$$I = 1$$
$$V = 5$$
$$X = 10$$
$$L = 50$$
$$C = 100$$
$$D = 500$$
$$M = 1,000$$

That's all you need to know regarding the numerals. For the record though I will note that $\overline{V} = 5,000$, $\overline{X} = 10,000$, $\overline{C} = 100,000$, and $\overline{M} = 1,000,000$, but you will never encounter these greater numbers. Classic mathematicians could omit the superscript, knowing that the text would convey the right number.

Just two more points and you are a full-fledged Roman mathematician. In Roman arithmetic, when the larger number precedes the smaller number you add the two together: CX = 110, or MCI = 1101. When the smaller number precedes the larger number, you subtract. Thus: XC = 90, CMI = 901, and MIC = 1099. As an example, the clue may ask either in Roman, MCCC ÷ XX, or in decimal, 1300 ÷ 20. In either case, the answer 65 must be entered in Roman, LXV. One last example: XXXIV x XIX (34 x 19). The answer, 646, in Roman DCXLVI. (**Tip:** Roman crossword answers are rarely this complex.) Finally, if the same number is repeated, add them together: II = 2, III = 3, CC = 200, CCC = 300. These numerals may look great on a brass plaque or an academic diploma, but it is easy to see why the decimal system (Hindu-Arabic) won the mathematical wars.

As noted previously, puzzles will frequently contain one or two Roman numerals in their corpus of clues, but on occasion "Roman Numbers" will be the theme of the crossword, with such titles as : "As The Romans Did," or "When In Rome." Such themes are likely to go far beyond plain numbers and evoke witty whimsical responses such as :

Mr. _____ (squatty one) = V by V

Gross = XII dozen

Tales told by Scheherazade = The MI Nights

Finally, remember that kings and popes usually include a Roman numeral as part of their cognomina:

Legendary Norwegian king = Olav I

Emperor of India, 1910–1936 = George V

Originally, G.M. Sarto = Pius X

The entry may be tricky if the solution requires multiple numerals:

Father of Elizabeth I = Henry VIII

Successor of Pius IX = Leo XIII

Oddly, two Arabic numerals also lend themselves to this form of crossword trickery. The numbers one (1) and zero (0) are used on occasion to represent the letters "i" and "o" in the crossing words. A recent puzzle called for "50505 doubled." The answer, 101010 provided a series of "i's" and "o's" for the crossing words. In Roman, that would be $\overline{C}$MX, but you already knew that.

---

[1] Arnot, Michelle. *What's Gnu? A History of the Crossword Puzzle.* Vintage Books, 1981, "Foreword."

GRAND AVENUE by Steve Breen

71

Tag—You're Out

Tags, explanatory constructs, appear far more often than Roman numbers, in almost every puzzle and occasionally as many as ten in a single grid. Constructors use tags to modify or explicate a clue, and these constructs, usually abbreviations, all follow a colon, except for the tag "e.g." which follows a comma. Almost all tags are self-explanatory, though they may occasionally be deliberately confusing; even trickery may be involved. Constructors may also include a word or phrase in the clue (such as: small, shortly, in brief, for short, etc.) which serves in lieu of the tag, such as these examples for the tag abbreviation:

A short helper = Asst

A sergeant briefly = NCO

Life story in brief = Bio

In special situations, a constructor may create a tag to fit a rare or unusual circumstance:

A curse: Cajun = Gree gree

Notched: Bot = Erose

However, the tags which follow are the standard forms you are likely to encounter in your next crossword.

1. Abbr.—Abbreviation

The tag calls for an abbreviated answer:

Wall Street Organization: Abbr. = NYSE

Nutmeg state: Abbr. = Conn.

FRANK & ERNEST by Bob Thaves

Easy, but remember the alternative signals for abbreviations.
An abbreviated word in the clue:

Wall Street org. = NYSE

Amer. winter holiday = Xmas

And the use of the period:

Sunday lecture = Sermon

Sun. lecture = Ser.

Col site = Mountain pass

Col. site = Oh. (Ohio)

2. e.g. — Exempli gratia. — (to give an example)

The tag indicates that the clue (most often a single word) is a member of or part of a larger general category. Name that category:

Manx, e.g. = Cat

Sutherland, e.g. = Diva

NAACP, e.g. = Assn

Often the clue includes a word or phrase which substitutes for e.g.:

Fuji for one = Apple

Luna for instance = Goddess

Occasionally e.g. asks for another example of the clue itself:

Lock, e.g. = Tress

Assassin, e.g. = Bravo

3. Var. — Variant

The tag indicates that the spelling of the answer will vary from the standard. Supposedly, the variant spelling should appear in some dictionary as an acceptable second choice, but you are unlikely to find it in your home lexicon:

Old English letter: Var = Eth

Beef sausage: Var = Baloney

Ratite bird: Var = Emeu

4. Fr. : Ger.: Sp.: It.: Brit. etc.

The tag calls for a translation of a common English word into the language or country indicated. But be aware that the tag may refer to a language or a country, and the answer is not abbreviated unless the rule of agreement holds:

Beer: Fr. = Biere

January: Mex. = Enero

Oh wow: Ger. = Ach

TV: Brit. = Telly

The abbreviations for language or country are fairly obvious, but if you are stumped, refer to the abbreviation section in your desk dictionary.

5. Obs. — Obsolete

The tag calls for an obsolete word or term, a construct formerly standard but no longer used:

Agreement: Obs = Marry

Yours: Obs. = Thine

Once: Obs. = Erst (Constructors enjoy using the clue, "Once, once = Erst")

6. Arch. — Archaic

The tag calls for an obsolete or unused word or term, usually used deliberately for emphasis. While grammatically different from obsolete, in crosswords the difference is barely noticeable:

Frightened: Arch. = Afeared

Mug: Arch. = Tankard

Platter: Archaic = Trencher

Club: Arch. = Truncheon

7. Sl.—Slang

The tag calls for a slang answer, a word or term of non-standard, informal speech, often associated with a particular group:

Drug user: Slang = Doper

Useless car: Sl. = Clunker

Pin up: Slang = Cheesecake

8. Colloq.—Colloquial

The tag calls for informal talk, street language, or slang, the kind of dialogue which peppers the pages of contemporary novels:

I'm not going: Colloq. = I aint gonna go

Yes it's true: Colloq. = Yeah right

Don't crowd: Colloq. = Gimme space

Released: Colloq. = Sprung

9. Dial.—Dialectical

The tag calls for a regional variety of speech, or the language of a particular area:

I didn't _____: Huck Finn = Nuther

Bag: Dial. = Poke

Calf: Dial. = Dogie

Not "fer" = Agin

10. Comb. form—Combining form

The tag calls for a non-word form designed to combine with another form to create a word. Some of the forms are familiar:

lact (milk), hem (blood) and cide (kill), but most are totally unknown parts of words. The SCALAWAG recommendation is to skip it provisionally, and find as many crossing letters as possible until a possible solution presents itself:

Examine: Comb. Form = Scrut

Nostril: Comb. Form = Nari

Far: Comb. Form = Tel

Kiss: Comb. Form = Oscul

11. 1922 (or any date)

The tag obviously calls for a particular person, place, or occurrence as of that date. It is frequently used to distinguish a specific occurrence from previous or later happenings:

Stanley Cup champs: 1974 = NY Rangers

Vice President: 1836 = Van Buren

Hero of "The Big Sleep": 1946 = Bogart

Assassination victim: 1901 = McKinley

King Kong heroine: 1976 = Lange

12. Bible, or Shake., or Twain, or any other writing or writer

This self-explanatory tag calls for a quotation or a fill-in-the-blank answer from the source indicated:

". . . aye, there's _____": Shake = The rub

"How _____ is": Gleason = Sweet it

"_____stops here": Truman = The buck

". . . the rose _____": Bible = Of Sharon

13. Question mark

Perhaps not a tag in the usual sense, nonetheless the question mark appearing after a non-question clue is a most tag-like modifier. The mark is the constructor's warning to expect the unexpected. The answer will likely be a pun, an anagram, or some play on words rather than a straight dictionary definition. As puzzles get tougher, the constructor may not provide such a signal:

Leader in Mexican outerwear? = Poncho Villa

See red? = Owe

Dermatologist, sometimes? = Itch doctor

Sharp NH city? = Keene

Cubed roots? = Diced

Ones calling the shots?: Abbr. = RNs

Oink pad? = Sty

Passing concerns?: Abbr. = Tds

However, by a quirk that clearly demonstrates cross-wordery's eccentricity, a particular odd construction ending in a question mark asks for the exact reverse—not a pun, not an anagram, not the unusual, but a literal reading of the clue. Once constructors have conditioned their acolytes to seek for word-play, the solvers inevitably miss the obvious, the literal. When the question mark follows a common phrase or an idiomatic expression, the clue is seeking, usually, a literal answer:

Bring home the bacon? = Shop

Name of the game? = Baseball

Big deal? = Full house

Wipe the floor with ?= Mop

Standard pick-up line? = Get in

Small potatoes? = Spuds

Smell a rat? = Stink

It is high time? = Noon

Was not off one's rocker? = Sat

Windshield cleaner? = Wiper

Make a bundle? = Bale

Under cover? = Abed

Finally, if the clue is a straight question, the signal does not apply:

Who peeked? = Tom

Where is Paris? = Kentucky

14. Pref.—Prefix

15. Suf.—Suffix

Prefixes and suffixes require a lengthier exposition which follows.

The Fixes—Pre and Suf

14. Pref.—Prefix

The tag calls for an affix at the beginning of a word or word base to form a new word, or to adjust or qualify the meaning. Such prefixes as maxi, non, pre, re, and un are familiar constructs, but there are hundreds lesser known to most crossworders. In addition to the tag, the constructors may simply call for a prefix in the clue:

Prefix for mouth = Oro

Prefix for thrice = Ter

Prefix denoting quality = Iso

Or they may employ a battery of terms which call for a prefix such as: before, preceding, leading, prior to, etc., etc.:

Sitting before pose = Dis

Head of the troops = Para

Preceding form = Uni

Dextrous opener = Ambi

Indeed, such forms outnumber the use of the tag. However, the tag does appear frequently enough:

Earth: Prefix = Geo

Nine: Pref. = Enne

Great: Prefix = Meg

Winged: Pref. = Pter

15. Suf.—Suffix

The tag calls for an affix to be placed at the end of a word base or root to form a new word: tion, ing, ly, ness, ster, and a hundred others. As with the prefix, the constructor may ask directly:

Suffix for gang = Ster

Suffix for kitchen = Ette

Suff. for simple = Ton

More often, however, constructors employ substitutes for the tag such as: follower, in addition, ending, trailed by, etc.:

Super ending = Ior

Path trailer = Way

Hope follower = Less

Cigar tip = Ette

Or they may use the tag:

A killer: Suff. = Cide

Front of: Suffix = Head

Study: Suffix = Logy

A scene: Suff. = Scape

Caution: Be aware that betimes the constructor may deliberately confuse the issue by requiring a word rather than a suffix:

Cat chaser = Call

Sell follower = Out

Foot trailer = Loose

Any one of the multitude of prefixes and suffixes that enrich our expressive language may be the answer in your next crossword, but a round hundred or so are the likely candidates. The system assumes that in time, Scalawaggers will become familiar with these constructs and apply them post-haste to the grid. For a running start, SCALAWAG provides a list of probables. Bear in mind that the clues in the list may have a half dozen analogues. Take the suffix "Phile" for example, as shown in the list below. The meaning given is "Lover of" but it might also have read enthusiast, devotee, follower, affinity for, liking, etc.:

Prefix—Meaning
Mal = Bad, improperly
Matri = Mother
Multi = More than one
Nulli = Nothing
Ovi = Eggs
Poly = Many
Post = After
Pre = Before, prior to

Prefix—Meaning
Quasi = Seemingly
Re = Again
Son = Sound
Tele = At a distance
Trans = AcrossUn = Not
Vice = Deputy
Xeno = Foreign
Zoo = Animal

PREFIX—MEANING

Prefix—Meaning
Agro = Farming
Ambi = On both sides
Ance = (ancy, ence, ency)
     A state or quality of
Anti = Against, the reverse
Aqua = Water
Arbor = Trees
Arch = Chief
Bene = Good, well
Biblio = Book(s)
Bio = Life
Cardio = Heart
Chrono = Time
Cide = Kill
Contra = Against
Crypto = Secret

Prefix—Meaning
Cyan = Blue
Cyclo = Circle
Deci = Ten, one tenth
Dorsi = The back
Equi = Equal
Eroti = Sexual
Ex = Former
Geo = Earth
Graph = Writing
Hemo = Blood
Helo = Sun
Hepta = Seven
Hydro = Water
Ideo = Idea
Labi = Lips
Lip(o) = Fat

SUFFIX—MEANING

Suffix—Meaning
Able = Ability to do
Ade = An action, result
Ast = A person associated with
Ate = Adjectival ending
Chrom = Color
Cine = Cinema, film
Circum = Around
Cy = Abstract state, condition
Derm = Skin
Er, Or = One who, that which
Er, Est = Comparative,
     superlative
Ese = Inhabitant or language
Ess = Female
Ette = Feminine
Ful = Given qualities

Suffix—Meaning
Ing = Present participle
Ish = Indication of charac-
     ter, frequently negative
Ism = An action or result
Ist = An adherent
Itis = Disease, ailment
Less = Without
Lite = MineralLith = Stone
Logy = Study subject
Manic = Abnormality
Ness = State or condition
     (not the Loch)
Ose = Sugar
Ped = Feet
Phile = Lover of
Phobi = Fear of

Suffix—Meaning

S (es) = Plural

S = Third person singular
   present tense

Ship = A quality of

Ster = A person or thing
   associated with

Therm = Temperature

Wise = In a given way

Tags are easy. Just don't get caught off base.

SCALAWAG

SCALAWAG (Solving Crosswords A-Laugh-A-Way-A-Game) is a four-part system that provides a good measure of fun as solvers work their way across and down the grid. System is, perhaps, overly grandiose for a scheme as simple as SCALAWAG, but whatever you may wish to call it, it works.

Tenet One: Playing the odds.

The major tenet of SCALAWAG is to play the odds. As the gambling casinos of the world illustrate, they rake in millions by playing the tiny odds in their favor. Solvers may also win when holding odds of 90%, 80%, 70%, and perhaps even 60%. So, when a 70% decision hangs in the balance, don't hesitate. Slap the assumed answer or letters into the white boxes, in erasable ink of course. Most often these assumptions will relate to a prefix or suffix, so place those letters in as many boxes as possible as you move down and across the grid. Not too surprisingly, those few letters will offer hints to the crossing words in a remarkable number of instances.

Volubility = _ _ _ _ness

Thaw a second time = Re_ _ _ _

Get rid of rodents = De_ _ _

The system requires one element of discipline on the solver's part. The puzzler must remember that all such entries are on speculation, and subject to erasure. If you gambled wrong, hey, there's an eraser on the end of your pen.

Tenet Two: Brain storms.

Tenet one has a corollary: play your intuition. That spark of intuition comes at two different times during the game: a flash of inspiration as the puzzler reads the clue for the first time, and the surprising bolt of enlightenment when the solver returns to a clue after a series of washouts. Somehow, that initial flash of inspiration seems to be right most of the time, and there are scores of oral and written accounts on the occurrence of the latter phenomenon.

Tenet Three: Skulduggery.

SCALAWAG requires as full a knowledge of constructor craftiness, of wordsmith wiles, as possible. Of course, every solving system requires such awareness, but it is particularly important for Scalawaggers because the greater use of speculation requires a greater awareness of possible trickery.

Tenet Four: Tips.

SCALAWAG employs all the solving tips that have been devised since 1913. From Margaret Farrar on, editors and addicts have suggested a plethora of hints, ideas, suggestions, advice, and techniques to propel puzzlers to peak performance. All of those injunctions are part of the SCALAWAG arsenal.

TENET ONE: PLAYING THE ODDS

Plurals

Scalawaggers know that our language holds many plurals, such as men, geese, mice, data, aurae, children, and pence, but the odds are better than 80% that the call for a plural ends in an "s" (or "es" for words that end in ch, sh, s, x, z: patches, rushes, masses, foxes, blintzes). So do as Mr. Jinx, who calls his mouse friends Pixie and Dixie "meeses," and add that terminal "s" immediately. The "s" for plurals is so ingrained in our consciousness, constructors call for the "s" even when its use is more than dubious:

Acclaims = Eclats

Diplomatic Assets = Tacts

Balances = Poises

Third person singular, present tense verbs

An ending in "s" is guaranteed: (he) makes, marries, nurtures, sits, stands, etc. Slap an "s" in place.

Past tense

Again, English holds verbs such as strode, held, wept, sent, sought, felt, and spoke, but Scalawaggers confidently place an "ed" on the grid when asked for a past tense, knowing they will be right more than 70% of the time: opted, hoped, worked, tried, etc., etc. As noted previously, those three constructions (s in plurals, s for third person verbs, and ed for past tense) are such dead give-aways that crossword editors caution tyro constructors to shun them if at all possible. However, to a large extent it ain't possible.

Affixes (Prefixes and Suffixes)

Many other affixes, such as re, pre, un, anti, pro, er and or, ness, and less are also high on the positive odds gamble, and even novice Scalawaggers apply them boldly:

Re—If the clue in any way, shape, or form implies again—Prefix

Pre—Prior to—Prefix

Un—An implied negative—Prefix

Anti—Acting against—Prefix

Pro—Support, in favor of—Prefix

Er and Or—One who or that which—Suffix

Ness—A state or condition—Suffix

Less—Without—Suffix

Er—Any hint of more or less (comparative)—Suffix

Est—Any hint of most or least (superlative)—Suffix

This clutch of word forms is the beginner's bag of information. Veteran Scalawaggers may apply a score more of such fixes: ab, age, bi, ade, cy, demi, ex, ful, geo, ing, ism, maxi, mini, ology, per, semi, tele, ura, xeno, and zoo are examples of that extended list of entries.

Ly

The suffix "ly" requires special notice because it helps to provide the "A Laugh" in SCALAWAG. This adverbial/adjectival suffix meaning "a type of," "a characteristic," or "a quality" has risen to the crown of crossword comedy by virtue of its association with Tom Swifties, adverbial puns which have found their way into individual clues and occasional crossword themes. Tom Swift was the hero of a series of boys' novels in the early 1900's, whose speech was speckled with adverbial/adjectival puns. Crossworders have enjoyed these puzzle Swifties:

April is here laughed Tom _____ = Foolishly

"_____" said Tom disarmingly = Drop the gun

"I'll dig up the truth," muttered Tom _____ = Gravely

"_____" said Tom haltingly = I can't go on

"Don't go left," shouted Tom _____ = Forthrightly

"I'm on TV," said the chef_____= Childishly

"It's permanent press," said the saleswoman _____ = Ironically

Currently, Tom Swifties are a theme staple in the crossword community, and the "ly" is an easy suffix to remember.

Ine

The suffix "ine" also deserves special note. It appears in adjective forms such as feminine and masculine, in noun forms: medicine and concubine, in chemistry and halogens: nicotine and chlorine, but we encounter it most as a suffix for the animal kingdom: canine = dog, feline = cat, equine = horse, bovine = cattle, avine = bird, piscine = fish, ursine = bear, porcine = swine, caprine = goat, cervine = deer, vulpine = fox, murine = mouse, corvine = crow, ovine = sheep, leonine = lion, colubrine = snake, etc.

Veteran Scalawaggers develop a sense of probability in regard to all affixes, knowing when the odds favor the prompt response and when to wait for some crossing letters. That sixth sense comes with time, trial, and erasure, and is available to any puzzler who will walk the SCALAWAG way, tread the SCALAWAG track, gamble with the SCALAWAG game, and laugh with SCALAWAG luck.

TENET TWO: BRAIN STORMS

Little that is scientifically verifiable may be credited to inspiration, though the crossword anecdotal hot-line is rife with such reports. Almost every puzzler seems to have experienced that wild flash of recognition, either on a first reading or returning to a problem word after a breather. The return may come after a brief interval, when the solver goes on with the rest of the grid at hand, or a lengthy period such as overnight; the answer seems to leap off the page. From Margaret Farrar on, editors have recommended that solvers leave a difficult patch and return later for the solution. There is no laboratory explanation for this phenomenon, but as noted previously, the cruciverb community is replete with instances of its occurrence.

TENET THREE: SKULDUGGERY

How to recognize the tricks of the trade, the playful practices of the producers, the artifices of the architects, the conceits of the constructors, the wiles of the wordsmiths. The tricks and gimmicks applied by constructors number in the hundreds and one thing is certain; new crossword traps are created weekly. That certainty will continue to the end of crosswords. Thus, no definitive tabulation of these tricks can be produced, because it will be deficient tomorrow. However, a line-up of the common culprits, the usual suspects, is possible. Herewith that line-up:

Proper nouns

Since the first letter of any clue is always a capital letter, constructors use the device to conceal the answer:

Superior = Lake
Marsh = Mae
Pound units = Cantos
Bashful = Dwarf
Nets = Team
Mature = Victor
Wilder = Thorton
Pacific bird = Dove
Key opening = O say
Shore = Dinah
Frost = Poet
Chris craft = Santa Maria
Twist = Oliver
Butler = Rhett
Castle innovation = One step
Street on old TV = Della

Last name/First name

Constructors love to mislead by citing the last name disguised as a first name:

Arnold = Matthew
James = William
John = Elton
Thomas = Norman

And the reverse is also employed as a ruse:

Writer Gay = Talese
Author Wright = Morris
Novelist Washington = Irving

Where, outside of crosswords, have you read of an author cited by his first name, such as "novelist Ernest," meaning Hemingway? Put out your boy scout alert, "Be Prepared."

Noun/Verb

Constructors will deliberately provide a clue that will call for a noun when you are thinking verb, or a verb when you are thinking noun:

Goldbricks = Shirks
Stalk = Celery
Charm = Amulet
Figure = Cost
Name = Dub
Record = Annal
Keep Guard = Moat
Leaving time = Spring

Claws = Tears at

Saw on the small screen? = Television adage

Falls for a married woman = Niagara

Tip: To help distinguish between a noun or a verb, silently but thoughtfully bombinate the SCALAWAG "A-To" mantra. Using "record" as an example: mentally hum, "a record—to record, a record-to record, a record-to record . . ." Your answer should arise by the third repetition: a record = annal, entry, memoir; to record = tape, enter, write.

Obscure meanings

Since many, probably most, English words hold more than one meaning, many clues seek the most obscure, the most esoteric answer to seemingly common questions:

Low joints = Tarsi

Mail man = Armorer

Better = A Las Vegas habitué

Wire material = News

A sun shade = Eclipse

Reward a runner = Elect

Silly macaroni = Fop

Weighty measure = The law

Party line = Conga

Popeye's rival = KFC

Covered with evergreens = Pined

Socks, e.g. = Cat

Thaw = Détente

Luke was his disciple = Yoda

Certain pups = Tents

Spotted = Dappled

Had a row = Oared

Soft tissue = Kleenex

Canine caretaker = Dentist

Put dough in a pot = Ante

Abbr.

Some clues give an abbreviation and ask for a full word from that abbreviation. One such clue that appears repeatedly is Q.E.D. (four letters). Q.E.D. stands for "quod erat demonstrandum,"[1] so the answer could be either "quod" or "erat," but it is almost always "erat":

A bit of Q.E.D. = Erat

A part of C.I.O. = Congress

Pronouncement of D.O.A. = Dead

Most such clues are fairly simple, but occasionally there is a real stumper:

Part of N.M.S.Q.T. = Merit[2]

Bit of F.S.L.I.C. = Loan[3]

Allusion

As the puzzles get trickier, constructors use fewer direct synonyms and resort instead to indirection and allusion. So much so, that in some cases, it is difficult to deduce the clue from the wording, let alone the answer from the clue:

Throw into a tizzie = Rattle

If there should be = In case of

Here and there = Around

Mundane = Everyday

Lead pipe cinch = Snap

Like female compared to male = Deadlier

Total wipeout = Massacre

Morse recourse = SOS

This is fun = Whee

Getting off = Sending

A to Z = Gamut

Oppressive = Heavy

So what = Big deal

You swear = Promise

Grind = Rat race

Don't you recognize the voice = It's me

Mercy = I'll be

In good condition = Salable

Do perfectly = Nail

You mean this isn't = Oh oh

"Sorry, no can do" = Fraid not

The nerve = I never

Swell = Neato

Marbles, so to speak = Sanity

Way off target = All wet

Leases = Pays rent

Five in a row = Bingo

Will you look at that = I'll be

"Er. . ." = I mean

"What again!" = Oh no

Double trouble

Cryptic crosswords always inform the solver of the number of words in the solution. Not so for most American crosswords and, consequently, constructors confuse puzzlers with this stratagem:

Take care of = See to

Later = See ya

Alas = So sad

Beat it = Get lost

The second word is most frequently a short function word, a preposition modifying the main word, such as: on, up, at, and to.

Thought about = Slept on

Incite = Egg on

Squelches = Sits on

Enters = Leads on

Relax = Ease up

Shredded = Tore up

Enjoyed immensely = Ate up

Destroy in a way = Chew up

Determine = Get at

Clawed = Tore at

Suggest = Hint at

Finger = Point at

Entertaining = Open to

Originate, give _____ = Rise to

On account of = Due to

Threw off = Lied to

On occasion, the solution may be a short three word answer:

Me too = As am I

Having an advantage = One up on

Overtook = Got up to

Like most tutoring = One on one

Above board = Up and up

Miffed = In a pet

To underline the obvious, when the clue denotes "phrase," the answer will be multi-worded.

Poesy

Poor poesy has had more questionable words foisted upon it than the Ark held beasties:

Upbeats in poesy = Arises

Begin to poets = Ope

Dark complexioned in poesy = Swarth

Cave to poets = Antre

Unfold in poesy = Ope

Huge to poets = Enorm

Yore in poesy = Eld

Brush up your balladry!

Kind of/Sort of

A favorite clue for constructors reads "Kind of" or "Sort of" (sometimes "Type of"). In the great majority of cases, the constructor is seeking a current expression, a witty phrase, or a common statement rather than a variety of whatever:

Kind of call = Mating

Sort of steps = Measured

Kind of dust = Star

Kind of storm = Barn

Sort of tale = Tall

Kind of wolf = Lone

Sort of ear = Tin

Kind of story = Some old

Deadly kind of race = Arms

Kind of campaign = Smear

Nonetheless, to keep solvers on their toes, constructors will throw in a true variety clue:

Kind of dog = Pom (rather than = Hot)

Kind of hat = Fedora (rather than = Old)

And on some occasions it may be difficult to say which of the two is present:

Kind of column = Loss

Sort of cupboard = Corner

Kind of heating = Solar

As noted, "Kind of/Sort of" is a popular practice. More than once I have encountered it eight times in a single puzzle, and one constructor used it a full ten times in a Sunday-sized puzzle.

Crosswordese

To cruciverbalists, crosswordese means the words and names that crop up repeatedly, such as ankh, ein, ern, ete, emu, lee, obi, Ono, oda, opah, etc. For Scalawaggers, however, the term refers to the unusual, bizarre, gonzo, outré answers supplied by constructors. Puzzle making and editing are difficult pursuits, so we may forgive most of these oddities. However, a basic rule of crosswords says, "No made-up words." Sometimes though, constructors push that principle over the precipice. All of these examples are taken from highly respected sources. I swear:

Advocate of status quo = Stand patter

Angry one = Fumer

Ascent = Upgo

Assented = Yessed

Base security = Safeness

Behaves shyly, old style = Coys

Biased in choice = Unrandom

Broadcaster = Airer

Called attention = Hoyed

Consolidated = Oned

Cruelty = Savagism

Destitute person = Needer

Destroy the spirit = Unsoul

Dispenser of pills = Doser

Driver of small horses = Ponier

Follow the sun = Westing

Guarded = Sentried

Idols = Baalim

Ill-fated glass house resident = Stoner

Immensity = Bigness

Indigent one = Needer

Intent readers = Porers

Irritating = Iring

Like a draft animal = Oxy

Making angry = Iring

Minor poem = Odelet

More depressed = Mopier

More fitting = Apter

More under the weather = Iller

Move shrubbery = Rebush

Neil Simon, e.g. = Comedist

Newcomer = Greeny

Not observed = Uneyed

Occupies = Busies

Of a former Venetian ruler = Dogal

Of a heavenly body = Cometic

Of an epoch = Eral

One waiting in ambush = Lier

One with trained eye = Seeer

Precipitated, old style = Snew

Private student = Tutee

Prosperity = Fatness

Remove a wrapping = Unlap

Rough = Untender

Send upward = Ensky

Shone = Rayed

Small paid notice = Adlet

Small ropes = Cablets

Soften; disarm = Unsteel

Specified amount = Unitage

Stage assistant = Cuer

Start a certain trip = Embus

Symmetrized = Evened

Tasted = Palated

Tidied up, old style = Neated

United = Oned

Unity = Oneness

Unwrote = Erased

Watcher = Eyer

Withdraw a request = Unwish

Withered conditions = Seres

Without aches = Unsore

Word before goose, gull or seal = Rosss

To wit—To woo

Wily, wise wordsmiths sometimes woo us with wonderful
Wildelike witticisms. Wake up your whimsy:

Like Modigliano's reclining nude = Shiftless

Deduce a refusal = Inferno

Answer to question, "Me goose?" = Uganda

Air apparent = Smog

Why is it wrong to whisper = Because its not aloud

What was said when Kitty awakened = Catsup

Miss Tucket = Nan

Worthless loafer = Odd shoe

Heavenly butter = Aries

Summer snake = Adder

She's as good as a mile = Miss

Closing bid = Adieu

City to avoid in Kansas = Dodge

Wildebeest country = Gnuengland

Sock exchange = Bout

How actress Woods dresses = Nattily

Day break = Nap

Italian bread = Lire

A man of morals = Aesop

A tall story = Attic

What towser has = One r

Bovine comment = Moo

Series opener = Ess

Parade month = March

First mate = Eve

"Got milk" request = Meow

Old jug = Sing sing

Some fishermen = Liars

Before many cooks = Too

Back burner = Sun

Potential queen = Pawn

Blah, blah, blah = Etc.

Origin of a drive = Tee

Bridge call = Ahoy

It has Swiss banks = Aare

Lofty groups = Choirs

Sites of unplanned visits = Er's

Neckline = Lasso

Big cheese in Greece = Feta

J.P. Office = Hitching post

Molding by gosh = Ogee

Dairy outlet = Udder

These jests are a bit baffling, but they provide not only an "Aha"
response but also a "Haha."

Abrn.

Those four invented letters stand for abbreviation, cross-wordese style. Constructors have decreed that any combination of three letters, sometimes four, truly stands for some English word, and they prove it in their grids. All these clues called for an abbreviation:

Metric measures = Cls

Like an envelope at the P.O. = Sld

Railway part = Trk

Bus rider's scrip = Tfr

However = Tho

Part of Congress = Hse

Prepared for mil inspection = Gid

U.S. political group = SLP

Signs table = Zod

One who establishes = Fndr

Press run of a book = Ptg

Radon location = PPI

Most of the UK = Gtbr

Morocco covered books = Edls

Very old = Anc

Puget and others = Sds

Percussion instrument = Xyl

Border = Marg

Shakespearean title = Ayli

If you add chemical endings (ane, ene, ine, one, ade, ede, ide, ode, etc.), to those answers and the equally common request for an academic degree, which may be any combination of three letters on the assumption that somewhere in the United States there exists a degree granting institution that will offer a BCE, a DFC, or an MLS, and on top of all these, the increasing number of clues requiring a noun, verb, or adjective ending, the solver is forced to a single conclusion: constructors can create an answer that will show any three letters of the English alphabet in succession.

Hidden definitions

Constructors delight in designing questions to delude decipherers with clues concealing connotations—quite cryptic:

1, 2 or 3 = Arabic numeral

Gives a PG = Rates

"i piece?" = Dot

Father time is = Clockwise

Separating membranes = Septa

Ringer relative = Leaner

_____; Abbr = Neg

Tip: Faced with a clue that defies definition, move on to find crossing letters. When the answer finally appears, the universal reaction is a slap on the forehead and an unspoken, "Darn, that is so simple, why couldn't I think of it."

Spelling versus meaning

Many American-English words are similarly spelled, but vary widely in meaning and often in pronunciation. A notorious case in point is "flower," meaning river. Other such azygous words which appear in our game are: butter, row, bow, adder, summer, glower, contract, address, lead, shower, project, tower, and scores more. **Tip:** Try an alternate pronunciation, that works much of the time, and stay alert.

It

A constructor's favorite is the "it" clue—it can, it may, it should, followed by an adjective. **Tip:** Find the noun that fits that adjective:

        It can be hot = Potato
        It comes with a battery = Assault
        It should be sweet = Corn
        It takes two = Calling birds
        It comes in a case = Stair
        It may be deferred = Hope
        It should be sterling = Worth
        It can thicken = Plot
Variant form: Agatha Christie was one = Dame

When the subject is plural, the "it' becomes "they:"

        They may be bitter = Ales
        They're often paid = Dues
        They may be grand = Slams
        They should be miserable = Culprits
        They can be helpful = Indices
        They may be drawn = Baths
        They can be rolled = Oats
        They always have titles = Nobles
        They're sold in lots = Used cars

That's in a name

Celebrities are a pet topic of constructors and at least one is sure to star in your next grid. However, crosswords are also the last refuge of non-celebrities whose induction into the crossword hall of remembrance rests solely on the peculiarity of their names. Thus, wholly forgettable characters may share equal crossword billing with real stars if their names provide special relief for puzzle makers. Among the hundreds of crossword luminaries and the undistinguished whose names are grist for the constructor's mill, particular places are reserved for the curiously yclept. That's what a name can do:

James Agee	Gatti Cassazza
Anouk Aimee	Coco Chanel
Desi Arnez	Lon Chaney
Adele Astaire	Oona Chaplin (O'Neill)
Tai Babilonia	Cyd Charisse
Enid Bagnold	Chevy Chase
Theda Bara (and the other	Noah Chomsky
glitterati of the silents and	Sandra Dee
early talkies: Renee Adoree,	Isak Dinesen
Vilma Banky, Edna Best,	Joanne Dru
Clara Bow, Lillian and	Wyatt Earp
Dorothy Gish, Elissa Landi,	Abba Eban
Nita Naldi, Pola Negri,	Taina Elg
Irra Petina, Lya De Putti,	Stu Erwin
Vera Vague, Pearl White)	Mia Farrow
Yul Brunner	Redd Foxx
Tia Carrere	Zsa Zsa Gabor

Zona Gale

Asa Gynt

Che Guevara

Uta Hagen

Signe Hasso

Ima Hogg (many puzzlers
   believe she has a sister Ura)

Erica Jong

Elia Kazan

Estes Kefauver

Etta Kett

Aga Khan

Eartha Kitt

Eda Le Shan

Estee Lauder

Mao Tse Tung

Anita Loos

Anais Nin

Tom Mix

Yoko Ono

Ara Parseghian

I M Pei

Zasu Pitts

Ayn Rand

Eero Saarinen

Bidu Sayao

Greta Scacchi

Talia Shire

Elke Sommer

Yma Sumac

Kiri Te Kenawa

Rip Torn

Liv Ullmann

Leon Uris

Elie Wiesel

Pia Zadora

Twisty Twins and Tricky Trines

Constructors use similar spellings, geographical proximity, related families, homophones, and near synonyms to create a degree of uncertainty for many puzzlers. The list is in reverse order with the entry first, the clue second. Videlicet:

Aa = Small river of northern France

Aare = River of north and central Switzerland

Aire = River of Yorkshire England

Altai = Mountains of Mongolia

Urals = Mountains of Russia. Border between Asia and Europe

DCM = British military medal, Distinguished Conduct Medal

DSC = American military medal, Distinguished Services Cross

DSO = British military medal, Distinguished Services Order

Ecto = Outside

Ento = Inside

Edh = Old English letter

Eth = Old English letter, variant spelling

Anoa = Wild ox

Gnu = African antelope

Ibex = Wild goat

Oryx = African gazelle

Tora = African antelope

Topi = African antelope

Zebu = Indian ox (not to mention ariel, bongo, okapi, eland, and a dozen other wild grazers)

Ares = Greek god of war

Mars = Roman god of war

Eros = Greek god of love

Amor = Roman god of love

Lees = Wine sediment

Marc = Residue of pressed fruit

Ras = Cape or headland

Ria = Narrow inlet or creek

Lethe = River in Hades whose waters cause forgetfulness

Styx = Principal river of the underworld to early Greeks

Eos = Greek goddess of the sky and dawn

Ops = Roman goddess of plenty and fertility

Scarcely = In a sparse manner, only just

Sparsely = In a scant manner, few scattered

Ani = Black cuckoo

Anil = Indigo, blue dye

Anile = Old woman

Aril = Seed pod or covering, sometimes seed

Carat = Jeweller's weight measure

Caret = Insertion mark for printed or written matter

Manet = Regarded by many as the major impressionist painter

Monet = Regarded by many as the major impressionist painter

Alpaca = Andean Ruminant

Guanoco = Andean Ruminant

Llama = Andean Ruminant

Vicuna = Andean Ruminant

Sora = An American bird

Hora = A circle dance

DNA = Nucleic acids, usually the bases of heredity

RNA = Nucleic acids that control cellular chemical activities

ABC = Enter the "B" and wait for crossing letters

CBS = Enter the "B" and wait for crossing letters

NBC = Enter the "B" and wait for crossing letters

PBS = Enter the "B" and wait for crossing letters

Disc = Variant spelling of "disk"

Disk = Appears less frequently than "disc"

Mall = Urban shopping center (**Tip:** Enter the "ma")

Mart = Urban shopping center (**Tip:** Enter the "ma")

Ret = To soak

Tet = Vietnamese holiday. Occasionally, variant of Hebrew Teth

Fir = Evergreen tree, usually American

Yew = Evergreen tree, usually European

Desert = Desolate sparsely settled area

Desert = Personal quality deserving a reward or punishment (just deserts)

Dessert = A course, usually sweet and usually served at the end of a meal

Ala = In the style of

Par = An accepted standard

Per = For each, a piece, by means of, through

Via = By way of, through the medium of, and by means of

Adapt = To make fit
Adept = Proficient, expert
Adopt = To take by choice

Gray = Most often the color between black and white
Grey = Most often a name as in Zane or Lady _____

Epode = A form of ode
Ode = A lyric poem

Tad = A small child, usually a boy
Tot = A small child
Lad = A young man or boy

Eremite = A religious recluse
Hermit = A recluse, usually religious

Oder = River of Germany chiefly in Hesse
Eder = River of central Europe

Otho = Roman Emperor
Otto = German King
Otto = Preminger

Alewife = A herring
Ale wife = A pub keeper

Prau = Indonesian sail and paddle boat
Proa = Variant of "prau" but appearing more frequently
Saic = Levantine boat (ketch)

Argosy = A large ship or fleet of ships
Armada = A fleet of war ships

Age = A period or length of time
Eon = A long long period of time
Era = A period of time, usually memorable

ILA = International Longshoremen's Association
ILO = International Labor Organization (UN)

Ana = A collection of anecdotes or memorable sayings
Ena = Oft cited Spanish Queen
Ina = Balin or Claire
Ona = Munson
Una = Merkel

Etage = Floor of a house (1st floor, 2nd floor, etc.), story
Etape = March, a day's march, occasionally a stage

Areola = Colored ring (as about a nipple), a small open space
Areole = A round area on a cactus
Aureole = A radiant light above the head, halo (alternative spelling aureola)

Rial = Near eastern monetary unit
Riel = Near eastern monetary unit
Riyal = Near eastern monetary unit

Agate = Type size
Elite = Type size

Fran = Ollie's friend
Stan = Ollie's friend

Abele = White poplar
Aspen = Poplar, also a white poplar

Eire = The old Ireland
Erin = The emerald isle

Hyper = Prefix—excess, too much
Hypo = Prefix—under, below normal, not enough

Macro = Prefix—very large, great
Magn = Prefix—very large, great
Mega = Prefix—very large, great
Maxi = Prefix—very large, great

Micro = Prefix—small, tiny
Mini = Prefix—small, tiny

Scope = Suffix—a specific scene
Scope = Suffix—an observation instrument

Ree = A Pawnee Indian
Ree = A female ruff (normally, reeve)

Petal = Part of a flower
Sepal = Part of a flower

Golf = Club sport
Polo = Club sport

Esne = Slave
Helot = Slave
Peon = Slave
Serf = Slave

Evens = Opposite of odds
Ends = Partner of odds

Orr = Bobby, Boston Bruins hockey, player, defenseman
Ott = Mel, NY Giants outfielder

Acre = Square foot measure of land
Are = Square yard measure of land
Area = A section of land

Smee = Pirate
Smew = Goose, duck
Snee = Large knife (snickersnee)

Toile = Twill weave fabric
Voile = Fine sheer fabric

Roam = To wander
Rove = To wander

97

Demi = Half
Hemi = Half
Semi = Half

Nice = French city
Nice = Pleasant, kind, respectable

In re = Regarding
As to = Regarding
Anent = Regarding

Lariat = A lasso
Lasso = A lariat
Noose = A lasso, occasionally
Reata or riata = A lariat or a lasso

RNs = Hospital workers
MDs = Hospital workers
Drs. = Hospital workers

Ino = (Leucothea) Daughter of Cadmus
Ion = Son of Apollo
Iole = Captive and lover of Hercules

Apse = Part of a church
Nave = Part of a church

Align = To straighten
Aline = To straighten

Bren = British gun
Sten = British gun

Enure = Variant of inure
Inure = To accustom, to accept

Aleut = Alaska native
Inuit = Alaska native

Eft = Newt (Immature)
Newt = Salamander, adult eft
Triton = Newt

Lana = Turner
Tina = Turner

TENET FOUR: TIPS

A tip is a gratuity, a point, a tilt, and an extremity; but in SCALAWAG a tip is a hint, a suggestion, an instruction, a word-to-the-wise word seeker. Some tips have been provided earlier; here are a few remaining bits of advice.

Q, U, etc.

A simple tip with a surprisingly good hit rate: if an uncovered letter U is showing, look for a preceding Q, and of course if a Q is showing, add a following U immediately. Secondly, if U is the initial letter try an N as the second letter; that combination is a recurrent crossword couple. And if a U is the penult, try a P as the terminal letter to see if the word "up" provides a solution.

In similar fashion, if an O occupies the last white square, see if a preceding T, for the word "to," will click. Veteran Scalawaggers also gamble on common suffixes, such as ing, ment, tion, ian, ter, ence, ster, etc. If you have one letter in the appropriate square, see if the others follow.

N.E.S.W.

N.E.S.W. are not only the points on the compass, they are also the seating arrangement for bridge games. The word behind the abbreviation may conceal a proper noun:

    North = Oliver
    East = Edward
    South = Robert
    West = Rebecca

Contemporary

An often used clue calls for a contemporary of the individual named in the clue. The answer requires not only a person living during the same time period, but also one engaged in a similar occupation, activity, or office. That is, an actor in the clue calls for an actor in the entry, a poet for a poet, a pol for a pol, etc., etc. Another example of agreement.

    Frost contemporary = Auden
    Broun contemporary: Abbr. = F.P.A.
    S.B. Anthony contemporary = C. C. Catt.
    Theda's contemporary = Pola

Half a

A clue calling for half a something is seeking an entry (usually half of two words) in which both parts are spelled identically:

    Half an African fly = Tse (Tsetse)
    Half a dance = Cha (Cha-cha)
    Half an African talisman = Gri (Grigri)
    Half a Philippine city = Ilo (Iloilo)
    Half a drum = Tom (Tom-tom)
    Half a cheerleader accessory = Pom (Pom pom)
    Half a guffaw = Har (Har har)

Analogy

The odd looking configuration A:B::C: _____ = ? only looks difficult. In fact it is one of the easiest clues to solve. It simply states, A is to B as C is to D:

    Hand:Arm::Foot: _____ = Leg
    Pear:Tree::Blackberry: _____ = Bush
    Sock:Foot::Glove:_____ = Hand
    Venus:Love::Mars: _____ = War

Run the alphabet

When a solution is lacking one, two, or even three letters, running all the letters of the alphabet in a blank square often produces the "Aha" effect. For instance, when stuck with the configuration, O_ _ U _ T, run the alphabet in the second white box; OA_ U_T—not likely, OB_U_T—no, OC_U_T—yes, looks like OCCULT.

Double check

On occasion, your crossword dictionary will not provide an answer, but will suggest a second word as a possible synonym. Check that second word in the crossword dictionary and you may find your answer.

Scholarly = ? (8 letters)

The dictionary does not provide a word that fits, but does show Learned. Learned shows Profound which fits, thus:

Scholarly = Learned

Learned = Profound

Scholarly = Profound

Work = Task

Task = Chore

Work = Chore

Careful, careful!

Read the clue carefully. Many a time have I been stuck for a period because I read Home for Horne, or beach toys for beach boys, or haggard for laggard. Even more important, print carefully; avoid the stymie. Make sure your P's don't look like D's, your E's like F's, your C's like G's. Don't take your N's for H's, your V's for U's, or your M's for N's. In addition to a simple misreading, which may delay the solution for a considerable time, SCALAWAG contends that there is more here than meets the eye or there is more here that meets the eye. For just as the world recognizes hand-eye coordination, the instinctive hand reaction to a moving object, SCALAWAG contends, with no scientific evidence whatever, but with a host of empirical observations, that brain-eye coordination also occurs. Distinct printing may allow the brain to read "instinct" from "_NS_I_CT", or "coordinate", from "C_OR_ _N_TE."

Before you start to sneer and guffaw, check this related commentary on brain-eye coordination which circulated on the Web during 2003 and 2004. The note about research at Cambridge University is bogus, but the brain-eye coordination is very real in the great majority of cases in English. The E-comment read, "Aoccdrnig to a rscheearch at Cmabrigde Uinervtisy, it deosn't mttaer in what oredr the ltteers in a wrod are, the olny iprmoatnt tihng is taht the frist and lsat ltteer be at the rghit pclae. The rset can be a total mses and you can sitll raed it wouthit porbelm. Tihs is bcuseae the huamn mnid deos not raed ervey lteter by istlef, but the wrod as a wlohe." Amzanig huh?[4]

Across versus down

American puzzlers are accustomed to reading across, left to right. If a down word stays unfinished, try writing the available letters across to see if that sparks a brain-eye coordination.

Sentence it

When a simple synonym is elusive, try the clue word in a sentence and discover a word that agrees:

Fashion = ?(4 letters)

It is the current fashion.

It is the current mode.

Fashion = Mode

Rampart = ? (4 letters)

We stood on the rampart.

We stood on the wall.

Rampart = Wall

Repeaters

Repeaters, known as "crosswordese" to all non-scalawag puzzlers, are the port of last resort for constructors. These overly repetitious words and names number by the dozens, are usually short, vowel heavy locutions, and succor the constructor when all else fails. Emu, ere, ern, ete, lee, and oda have already been noted, and there are a hundred others, such as: alb, aloe, baa, erat, esse, gee, ibo, Isis, lea, nil, neo, obi, psi, sago, sen, tabu, wadi, yak, and zwei just to name a score in addition to those noted earlier.

Tip: Get to know these repeat offenders—make a list, memorize them.

Foreign traps

Gender plays a small role in English, and even less now that we accept social correctness and drop gender defining affixes. Thus, actor now substitutes for actress, chair for chairman, twirler for majorette, and pilot for aviatrix. However, the animal world still maintains those distinctions: lioness, bitch, cow, vixen, hen, ewe, mare, etc. Remember, however, that almost all the European languages that show in crosswords maintain gender differentiation:

Friend: Fr. = Ami
Friend: Fr. = Amie
Friend: Sp. = Amigo
Friend: Sp. = Amiga
Friend: Ger. = Freund
Friend: Ger. = Freundin

Article

Article, by itself, is an oft used clue meaning: the, a, or an. However, be wary of a hint at a foreign language thus requiring a translation:

Article in Le Temps = Une
A Bremen article = Der

Modifier

When the constructor adds a modifier to the final word, it is a signal that the answer should include that word to make sense. Most often the modifier is enclosed in parentheses, but sometimes not.

Rested (on) = Relied
Desires, with "after" = Lusts
_____ off (evaded) = Warded
Inspired with "up" = Fired
Closest (to) = Next
Hope (for) = Watch
Surround (in) = Close
Confronting with "to" = Facing up
Victimized with "on" = Preyed

Ascription

A clue that provides a partial quotation and the author of the quotation frequently notes that the author says A is B. What is A, or what is B:

". . . is a literary specialty": Twain = Weather
"The only thing we have to fear . . . ": Roosevelt = Fear itself
". . . is the perfect herald of joy": Shake. = Silence
"A good breakfast, but an ill supper": Francis Bacon = Hope

Desperation

When desperation strikes the constructor, anything goes. For instance, who can argue with a sound:

Rasping sound = Scroop
Murmuring sound = Curr

Insect sound = Churr

Shrill, trilling sound = Chirr

Bird sound = Tiralee

or a name:

Girl's name = Nida

Girl's name = Firna

Tip: Faced with desperation, move on and wait for lots of crossing letters.

Negation

Almost every word indicating negation begins with the letter n: not, neither, no, nil, nix, none, nay, nary, null, etc., etc. You are very safe responding to a negative type clue with an initial n.

Some

Every clue that calls for some is requesting a plural:

Some are fancy dives = Gainers

Some are GPs = MDs

Some say welcome = Mats

Some hats = Felts

Gh

If the letters GH are uncovered to the left (or up) of an incomplete entry: (_ _ _ gh), you run a very low risk gamble dropping the letters "OU" before that pair: bough, rough, through, thought, though. Nonetheless, keep your eraser handy for the small possibility that the clue may call for an "AU" instead: caught, laugh, fraught; or an "I": fight, mighty, or some similar vowel combination: freight, straight. If the GH is uncovered to

the right or down, the insertion of the letter "T" is a sure bet: fought, laughter, bought, taught, weight, height.

Teams

Finally, by a quirk of nomenclature, the great majority of professional ball team names end in s, with some few exceptions, such as the Utah Jazz and the Boston Red Sox: Yankees, Giants; Knicks, Lakers; Dolphins, Rams; Rangers, Bruins. In the NFL all 32 teams' names end in s. Major League Baseball, 34 names, 32 end in s. The exceptions, the Boston Red Sox and the Chicago White Sox, but they simply don't know how to spell socks. The NHL, 30 appellations, 27 ending in s. (exceptions: Avalanche, Wild, Lightning). The NBA, 29 cognomina, three s-less: Jazz, Heat, Magic. The same name peculiarity pertains to collegiate teams, as a puzzle in *Games*[5] magazine confirms. The puzzle listed forty eight varsity teams: forty three names ended in s. However, the women are the exception to the rule; only 4 of 13 WNBA monikers hold a final s. Despite the WNBA, when faced with a team name clue, inserting that ultimate s is a very low risk gamble.

I'm sure I have missed some tips, and there are new ones being coined weekly. To keep up to date on such hints, check out my website: bearklaw@dcn.org

Stay sharp, but remember, this is a game, so go for the fun.

---

[1] That which was to be proved.

[2] National Merit Scholarship Qualifying Test

[3] Federal Savings and Loan Insurance Corporation

[4] For a scholarly explication of the comment, check: http://www.mrc-cbu.cam.ac.uk/personal/matt.davis/cambridge

[5] "Team Players." *Games*, November, 2004, p. 29

Offspring and Sisters

The rage for crosswords has helped spawn a pair of word-play relatives. This brief account of those relatives won't help you solve any puzzles, so you may take a pass on this section if you wish. But you will miss some good stuff.

THE DOUBLE-CROSTIC

Tony Augarde, the famed British games guru, shows a bit of homeland prejudice in his otherwise commendable guide to word games.[1] He fails to point out that the three most popular, most celebrated word games of the 20th century are crosswords, Double-Crostic, and Scrabble, all American inventions. In addition, American crosswords get two pages while all the rest of that chapter, eleven pages, is devoted to English cryptic puzzles. Scrabble does just a mite better, but Double-Crostic, the second most popular word game of the century, is merely a one paragraph after-thought on crosswords. What mightbe excused as an oversight in the first edition of the *Guide*, (1986) though Double-Crostic had been around for 50 years, is inexcusable for the second edition, (2003), for the

An early Double-Crostic

Double-Crostic had soared to extraordinary popularity and importance in the two decade interval between editions. Ten pages for Palindromes, one paragraph for Double-Crostic!

Augarde's apparent prejudice is even more telling, since the history of the Double-Crostic is fascinating.[2] Elizabeth Kingsley, a former teacher and puzzler, attended her college reunion at Wellesley in 1933 and discovered that the undergrads were broadly versed in James Joyce, Gertrude Stein, and their contemporaries, but ignorant of older and classic authors. Elizabeth was appalled and determined to kindle their interest with a game promoting excerpts from major American and English authors, and to provide the author's name and the source of the quotation. Within six months she produced several score puzzles she dubbed Double-Crostic. The *Saturday Review* editors snatched the puzzles on sight, and even bought the rights to the name. The *Review* also commissioned Kingsley to produce a weekly Double-Crostic, the first of which appeared on March 31, 1934. Later, she constructed similar game sheets for Simon &

Schuster's serial publication and for *The New York Times*. Reportedly, she constructed 2,500 Double-Crostics over time and developed a fan following, including a score of eminent literary figures, unparalleled in its devotion in the history of puzzledom. Devotees across the country rallied to Queen Elizabeth and to her Double-Crostic Club, and rejoiced in her commentary in "The Crostic Club Column" which accompanied her puzzles.

Since Elizabeth, The Double-Crostic has spread across numerous publications: newspapers, magazines, and books; and has seen more than a score of editors at the helm. It has undergone several name changes. In the *New York Times* for instance, it started as the Double-Crostic, but three changes later it is known as the Acrostic (July 7, 1991). Today, Simon & Schuster use a slight variant; they issue four series of the Double-Crostic under the various subheadings of Crostics. Whatever the name, its popularity remains undiminished, second only to its intellectual forebear, the crossword. *The New Yorker* underlined that relationship and popularity. On November 29, 2004 they published an acrostic in exact imitation of the crossword puzzle they had run the previous year. (See page 25.)

Nine previously published cartoons with deleted caption words served as the clues. The missing captions were the entries.[3]

SCRABBLE

If Scrabble could be played in the daily local newspaper, it would probably rival Double-Crostic in popularity. However, the board game requires a competitor (though solitaire Scrabble is available) and thus, it is a less frequently pursued recreational form than the Double-Crostic. Scrabble owes its origin to the Great Depression of the 1930's.

In 1931, Alfred Mosher Butts, an unemployed Poughkeepsie architect, devised a boardless cardboard version of Scrabble he called Lexico. (The name went through several transmogrifications: Lexico, New Anagrams, Alph, and Criss Cross, before it emerged with that remarkable cognomen, Scrabble.) Butts' homemade products, about 200 total, were sold to friends, but he was twice refused a patent on his creation and, on several occasions, the game industry big-wigs rejected his design. In 1948 Butts gave manufacturing rights to James Brunot, for a royalty on each sale. Brunot was able to secure a copyright on December 1,

1948 and a trademark on December 16, but the making of the boards and tiles was still a family operation, and the Brunots could knock out only 12 puzzles an hour. In the first four years, just 2,251 games were bought and Brunot was losing money on each board. Discouraged, he was about to toss in his tiles when word of mouth provided a major sales boost.

Brunot persevered. The real bonanza however, was provided by Jack Strauss, chairman of Macy's department stores, who had played the game on vacation and requested a set from his toy department. When he discovered the store did not stock the game, he ordered it. The store promoted the game, and from that point, sales went through the clouds. By 1963, 6,000 sets a week were going out the door, and game companies scrambled for the rights to market. Sales were so heavy that purchasing agencies were rationed as to the number of sets they could receive regularly. Today, Scrabble is played in 121 countries, in 29 languages, on 100 million boards. Scrabble Clubs, more than 100, have sprouted all across the United States and elsewhere, keeping members up to date on contests, word data, and general information. The first international world championship Scrabble tournament was held in London in 1991, the second in New York in 1993, and on every second year thereafter in major cities across the globe. Today, hardly a day goes by without a Scrabble tourney somewhere in the United States. In 1991, Stefan Fatsis tried to capture the fanatic followers of the game in his book, *Word Freak*.[4] In 2003, a similar attempt was made by Scott Patterson in his documentary film, *Scrabylon*, and in 2004 a second docu-mentary, *Word Wars*[5] debuted at the Sundance Film Festival and was shown later on the Discovery Times channel as a compelling American cultural trend. The 2004 national United States championship finals (New Orleans) was televised nationwide by ESPN, and two major competing full length feature films are being planned for 2005–2006. There is little doubt that Scrabble has eclipsed Parcheesi, chess, and checkers as the most popular board game on the planet.

ANAGRAMS AND CRYPTOGRAMS

Though somewhat removed from crosswords, two other word games featured in magazines and newspapers, particularly in the local daily hometown press, deserve brief mention. Anagrams has a loyal following and as Augarde notes, it has been a part of English recreational word play since the Middle Ages.[6] Anagrams has been a mainstay of British parlor games for three centuries and is enjoyed today by thousands of Americans in such daily games such as Jumble.

Cryptograms or ciphers, another American innovation, doesn't even rate a one word mention in Augarde's *Guide*. Cryptograms is a relatively late comer to the game scene. It was developed in the early 1920's, and it led to the inauguration of the American Cryptogram Association, in September, 1929. Today, Cryptogram devotees find their daily portion in the feature pages under such titles as Cryptoquotes, Celebrity Cipher, and a large serving in *Games* magazine's Dszquphsbnt!

All these pastimes point to an insatiable love for words and wordplay, with crosswords leading the parade.

[1] Augarde, Tony, *The Oxford Guide to Word Games*. 2nd ed. Oxford University Press, 2003.

[2] For a fuller account than is possible here, see: Arnot, Michelle, *What's Gnu? A History of the Crossword Puzzle*. Vintage Books, 1981, pp. 142–163.

[3] *The New Yorker*, "The Cartoon Issue," November 29, 2004, pp. 140–141.

[4] Fatsis, Stefan. *Word Freak: Heartbreak, Triumph, Genius, and Obsession in the World of Competitive Scrabble Players*. Houghton Mifflin, 2001.

[5] Chaukin, Eric and Petrillo, Julian. *Word Wars: A Documentary*. 2004.

[6] Augarde, Tony. *Oxford Guide to Word Games*. 2nd Ed. Oxford University Press, 2003, pp. 80–93.

ST. NICHOLAS:

SCRIBNER'S
ILLUSTRATED MAGAZINE

FOR GIRLS AND BOYS

CONDUCTED BY

MARY MAPES DODGE.

VOLUME I.
NOVEMBER, 1873, TO NOVEMBER, 1874.

SCRIBNER & CO., NEW YORK.

The First Crossword—History Reenvisioned

Two points of historic pertinence have been noted earlier: 1—that crosswords was a descendant of the word square (p. 23), and 2—that the first crossword appeared in the December 21, 1913 pages of *The New York World's* Sunday FUN section (pp. 25–26). There is little dispute regarding point 1, but the question of WHEN the word square coalesced to the crossword has occasioned some question regarding point 2.

A current truism notes that if it looks like a duck, walks like a duck, and quacks like a duck, it must be a duck. But what if it walks like a duck, and quacks like a duck, but doesn't look like a duck—is it still a duck? At least one lexicographer says, "Yes." Martin Manser, a highly regarded author, wordmaster, and reference book editor—he has written or edited more than 70 reference books including dictionaries and thesauruses for major publishing houses as diverse as

the Oxford University Press, Zondervan, Macmillan, Thomas Nelson, and Penguin—wrote "that the earliest known crossword was a 9 by 9 Double Diamond published in *St. Nicholas*, for September 1875."[1] *St. Nicholas* was the premier children's magazine of the late nineteenth and early twentieth centuries, rivaled, perhaps, only by *The Youth's Companion*.[2]

Each month Mary Mapes Dodge, editor of *St. Nicholas*, included two or three pages of puzzles in "The Riddle Box" for the delight and challenge of her pre-teen and teen readership. The answers to the riddles and puzzles would appear in the following month's issue. Manser is referring to the "Double Diamond Puzzle" by Hyperion[3] with crosswordlike clues and wording such as "Across" and "Down," precisely similar to current crosswords. The answer, however, resembles an odd shaped word square rather than a current crossword.[4]

DOUBLE DIAMOND PUZZLE.

(LARGEST EVER MADE.)

ACROSS: 1. A consonant. 2. A household god. 3. Equaled. 4. Existing only in name. 5. Arched. 6. Taken by robbery. 7. Luxurious food. 8. Conducted. 9. A consonant.

DOWN: 1. A consonant. 2. A spigot. 3. To imitate for sport. 4. Pertaining to the side. 5. Filled to repletion. 6. Told. 7. Fruit much used for food in Arabia. 8. A color. 9. A consonant. HYPERION.

```
    S
   L A R
  M A T E D
 T I T U L A R
C A M E R A T E D
 P I R A T E D
  C A T E S
   L E D
    D
```

Other crossword fans have commented on that possibility and one aficionado, nicknamed Sergio, citing a similar but even earlier "Double Diamond Puzzle," takes an opposing view and labels that puzzle as "the true ANCESTOR of the crossword puzzle [emphasis mine].[5] The puzzle[6] and the answer[7] appeared some months earlier than Manser's candidate.

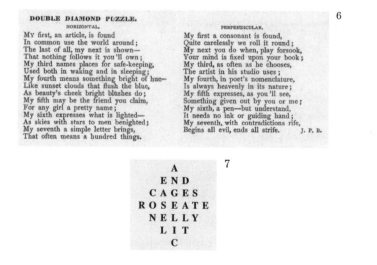

Sergio suggests a possible evolutionary track for the crossword, the final merging of the two puzzle forms (he mistakenly writes, "There is no 'Riddle-Box' for the April number"), and concludes that "the crossword puzzle ancestor is a variant

of the Diamond puzzles,"[8] He also refers to Roger Millington's assessment of the Diamond puzzles and agrees with Millington's notion that Arthur Wynne, the historically acknowledged first crossword constructor, knew and drew upon these earlier Double Diamonds.[9]

Indeed, Millington makes a strong case for such dependency for he asserts that "Wynne told his journalistic colleagues that he got the idea from children's magazines he had read as a child in Liverpool," and, probably, "*St. Nicholas* was among…magazines…published in Britain as well as in America."[10]

The same conclusion must be reached by any attentive reader, for Arthur Wynne was thirteen when these Double Diamonds appeared in 1875. The magazine was expressly designed for thirteen-year-olds, and Arthur must surely have been a youthful puzzler. The clues, as Millington notes, were crosswordish linguistically and were presented as "Across" and "Down." In addition, the pattern was a diamond shape, which Wynne later adopted for his own puzzles. All in all, too circumstantial to be merely coincidental.

Millington, however, has his own Double Diamond candidate for the first true ancestor, and incorrectly cites *St. Nicholas* for December 1880 as the source. The puzzle actually appeared in the December 1889 issue of the magazine. Millington goes on to note that "It is the earliest that I have come across using the now familiar Down and Across clues—although earlier examples may possible be discovered." Indeed, there were earlier examples, those already cited and such puzzles as those for December 1887 and October 1888. He writes that "It is tempting to think that the puzzle below is one that young Arthur sweated over as a boy."

11 12

DOUBLE DIAMOND

Across
1. In Chinaman.
2. A pert townsman.
3. An old word meaning the crown of the head.
4. The Indian name for a lake.
5. A prize given at Harvard University.
6. A masculine nickname.
7. In Chinaman.

Downward
1. In Chinaman.
2. A capsule of a plant.
3. A printer's mark showing that is interlined.
4. Men enrolled for military discipline.
5. A fibrous product of Brazil.
6. The first half of a word meaning very warm.
7. In Chinaman.

```
        M
      C I T
    P A L E T
  H O R I C O N
    D E T U R
      T I M
        A
```

Or, to show the Double Diamond and the answer as they originally appeared in *St. Nicholas*.

13

DOUBLE DIAMOND.

ACROSS: 1. In Chinaman. 2. A pert townsman. 3. An old word meaning the crown of the head. 4. The Indian name for a lake. 5. A prize given at Harvard University. 6. A masculine nickname. 7. In Chinaman.

DOWNWARD: 1. In Chinaman. 2. A capsule of a plant. 3. A printer's mark showing that something is interlined. 4. Men enrolled for military discipline. 5. A fibrous product of Brazil. 6. The first half of a word meaning very warm. 7. In Chinaman.

            H. AND B.

14

Cross-words: 1. Holly. 2. Tents. 3. Horns. 4. Dance. 5. Parry. 6. Fruit.
DOUBLE DIAMOND. Across: 1. M. 2. Cit. 3. Palet. 4. Horicon. 5. Detur. 6. Tim. 7. A. Downward: 1. H. 2. Pod. 3. Caret. 4. Militia. 5. Tecum. 6. Tor (rid). 7. N.
DOUBLE FINAL ACROSTIC. Fourth row (downward), Mistletoe; fifth row (upward), Xmas Story. Cross-words: 1. Palmy. 2. Choir. 3. Lasso. 4. Scott. 5. Foils.

Reaction to these Double Diamonds, as to whether they are precursors or embryonic versions of the crossword itself, seems to tilt in favor of precursor rather than a rudimentary form of our present black and white grid.

That's it. Your turn, ancestor or early crossword?

A CURIOUS SIDEBAR

A curious sidebar to these early puzzles is the issue of recognition of the term "crossword." That locution, usually spelled Cross-Word, appears throughout the puzzle pages of *St. Nicholas* from 1873 on, in relation to puzzles, but not to the symmetric grid we now associate with that verbalism. Even earlier, that very expression, regularly spelled Cross-words, appears so frequently on the puzzle pages of *The Riverside Magazine For Young People*, 1868–1870, that it is fruitless to cite single occurrences. Nonetheless, *The Oxford English Dictionary*, our foremost authority for the earliest appearance of an English word, lists 1914 for the first appearance of "cross-word, cross-word."[15]

Hey! Sir James Murray, wherever you are, make a note.

[1] Manser, Martin. *The Guinness Book of Words.* 2nd ed. Guinness Publishing Company, 1991, p. 128.

[2] An excellent history of *St. Nicholas* may be viewed at: http://flying-dreams.home.mindspring.com/nick.htm. "A Tribute to St. Nicholas."

[3] *St. Nicholas*, September 1875, p. 719.

[4] Ibid. October 1875, p. 784.

[5] http://www.cs.ubc.ca/spider/jhoey/xword/history.txt, p.1.

[6] *St Nicholas*, March, 1875, p. 327.

[7] Ibid. April 1875, p. 392.

[8] http://www.cs.ubc.ca/spider/jhoey/xword/history/txt, p.1.

[9] Ibid.

[10] Millington, Roger. *Crossword Puzzles: Their History and Their Cult.* Thomas Nelson Inc., 1974, p. 44. (Another decent history degraded by the lack of an index.)

[11] Ibid. p. 45.

[12] Ibid. p. 163.

[13] St. Nicholas, December 1889, p. 192.

[14] Ibid. January 1890, p. 279.

[15] *The Oxford English Dictionary.* 2nd ed. Clarendon Prss, 1989, Volume IV, p. 61.

Vale

Success in crosswords depends on three things: patience, perseverance, and perspiration. Well, you may not sweat solving crosswords, but it sounds good. The other two attributes you will definitely need in large supply. SCALAWAG veterans know that it takes stick-to-it-iveness to get the requisite expertise to solve the Sunday puzzles of our nation's newspapers, but such facility comes only after a long apprenticeship and frequent, frustrating flops. Stay patient and persevere. You will in time have a ragbag of repeaters at your beck; you will identify the personalities which pepper the puzzles; as you cry, "Aha," you will laugh rather than damn crosswordese; you will shout *ecce homo, dictum ac factum* to Roman numbers; you will, almost instinctively, sense when foolery is afoot; you will have a BBL. of answers for abbreviation queries; and you will be in the enlightened company of those who know that the metal or plastic tip to a shoelace is called an aglet. All these attainments and more come with patience, perseverance, and the system.

As recompense, you will be rewarded with mental acuity, reams of new information, nostalgic reunions, wonderful word-play, and more fun and enjoyment than a carton of cavorting kittens. But best of all, and perhaps unaware, you will be a player in one of the greatest games of all time: the continuance, the growth, the care, and the safekeeping of one of man's highest achievements, the glorious, unparalleled American-English language.

Go get 'em Scalawaggers.

Illustration Credits and Acknowledgments

Puzzle Answers

PUZZLE: PAGE 26

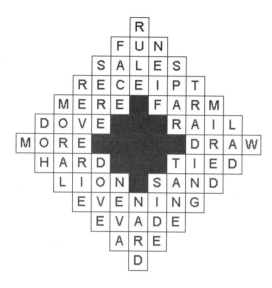

PUZZLE: PAGE 46

10 MISTAKES: Unsymmetrical grid; two 2-letter answers; LORE in the grid twice; ACROSS heading instead of DOWN; 56A: PUZLE misspelled; 50A: clue out of sequence; two 13D clues; 37D: phony clue; 47D: answer repeated as its clue; Shortz spelled Shorts

PUZZLE: PAGE 128

Index

by Barbara Ellen Lekisch

NOW IT'S YOUR TURN TO PICK UP THE PEN!

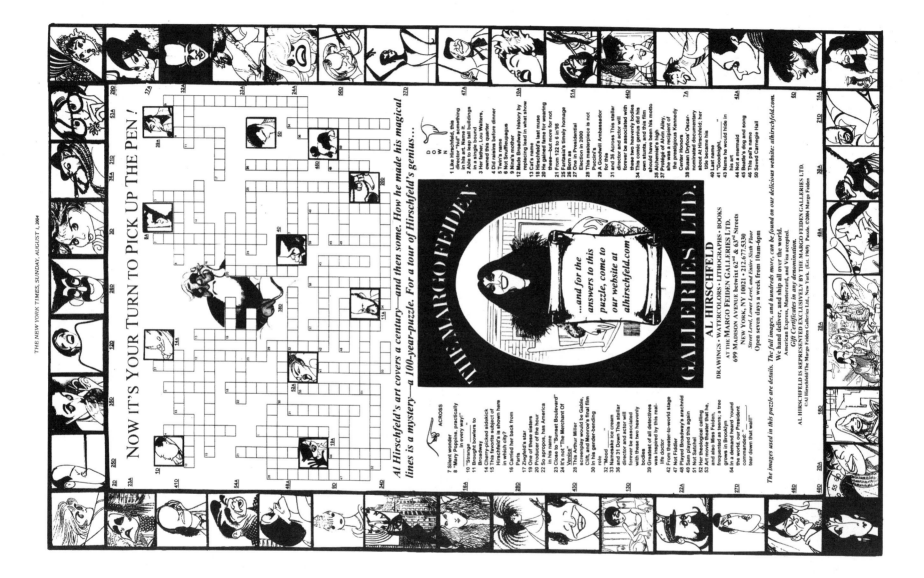

Al Hirschfeld's art covers a century—and then some. How he made his magical lines is a mystery—a 100-year-puzzle. For a tour of Hirschfeld's genius...

ACROSS

7 Silent wonder
8 "Mary Poppins, practically in every way!"
10 "Strange ___"
11 Brought bowlers to Broadway
14 Cherry-picked sidekick
15 This favorite subject of Hirschfeld is shown here in which city?
16 Carried her back from Paris
17 Ziegfeld's star
19 One of these sisters
20 Producer of the hour
22 So apropos, has America in his name
23 Close to "Sunset Boulevard"
24 It's not "The Merchant Of Venice"
28 This Arthur Miller screenplay would be Gable, Clift, and Monroe's final film
30 In his gender-bending role
32 "Mood ___"
33 Namesake ice cream
36 and 31 Down This stellar director and actor will forever be associated with these two heavenly bodies
39 Greatest of all detectives was inspired by this real-life doctor
42 From theater-to-world stage
47 Not Fiddler
48 Played Broadway's arachnid
49 Sam played this again
51 Not Satchel
52 Her theological calling
53 Art movie theater that he, and also Miss Feiden, frequented as teens; a tree grows in Brooklyn
54 In a demand heard 'round the world, our President commanded: "___ tear down that wall!"

DOWN

1 Like Hirschfeld, this director "hid" something in his art. Name it.
2 Able to leap tall buildings in a single bound
3 Her father, Lou Walters, owned this quarter
4 Did raisins before dinner
5 Twin's name
6 Not Snuffleupagus
9 Nina's mother
12 Made Broadway history by replacing lead in what show
13 Cat's name
18 Hirschfeld's last muse
20 He gained fame for wearing these—but no more for not
21 From 12½ to 5 in '90
25 Fantasia's timely homage
26 Born at
27 One in Presidential Election in 2000
28 This masterpiece is not Puccini's
29 A Goodwill Ambassador for this
31 and 36 Across This stellar director and actor will forever be associated with these two heavenly bodies should have been his motto
34 This comic genius did his own stunts, and this film
35 Alchemist's high
37 Protégé of Alvin Ailey, she was a recipient of the prestigious Kennedy Center Honors
38 Susan Dryfoos' Oscar-nominated documentary about Al Hirschfeld; her title became his
40 Last name
41 "Goodnight, ___"
43 Name he would hide in his art
44 Not a mermaid
45 Beatle's dog and song
46 This pal's name
50 Saved Carnegie Hall

Now It's Your Turn To Pick Up The Pen!

Sunday August 1, 2004

Solution:

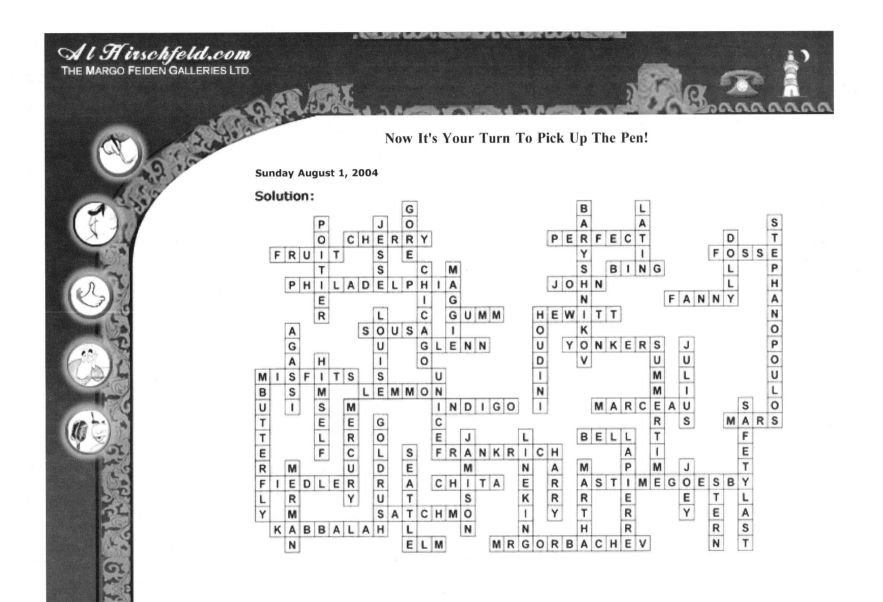

CROSSWORD LINUS

ACROSS

1. Peanuts character with a blanket
3. Lucy _ _ _ Pelt
6. Linus _ _ _ _ _ _ _ _ St. Paul
10. "_ _ Olde Mill"
12. Artist Judkins' initials (see base of statue)*
14. Peppermint Patty's friend
17. Capital of Minnesota
18. Santa's word
20. Opposite of down
22. Linus' blanket gives him this
26. Used by 23-down to clean the floor
27. Young contempory composer of Beethoven, Franz _ _ _ _ _

DOWN

1. Schroeder's Pest
2. Arrest a thief
4. Charles Schulz attended an _ _ _ school
5. Not off
7. Pd. or #
8. Per person
9. Observe with your eyes
11. Dine
13. Heroric story
14. Twelfth Greek letter
15. Alabama state abbreviation
16. Three letters meaning debt
17. Sally to Charlie or Lucy to Linus
19. Tag, you're _ _!
21. Linus Van _ _ _ _ _ _
23. Sponsor of crossword Linus: _ _ _ lab (see base of statue)**
24. Railroad, abbr.
25. _ _ _ or no answer

*A E
**E C O

PEANUTS © United Feature Syndicate, Inc.